Unafraid of the Sacred Forest

Unafraid of the Sacred Forest

The Birth of a Church in an African Tribe

Ronaldo Lidorio

and

ISBN 1-84550-235-3
ISBN 978-1-84550-235-5

10 9 8 7 6 5 4 3 2 1

Published in 2007
by
WEC International
Bulstrode, Oxford Road, Gerrards Cross, Buckinghamshire,
SL9 8SZ, England, Great Britain
www.wec-int.org.uk
and
Christian Focus Publications Ltd,
Geanies House, Fearn, Ross-shire,
IV20 1TW, Scotland, Great Britain
www.christianfocus.com

Cover design by Danie Van Straaten

Printed and bound by
Nørhaven Paperback A/S, Denmark

CONTENTS

Appendixes

Foreword

Unafraid of the Sacred Forest is a wonderful chapter in God's Story of redemption and transformation.

God used Ronaldo and Rossana Lidorio powerfully in this work of the Spirit in the Koni area of Ghana and I can testify to the truth of what Ronaldo and others have written. The Lidorios are dear friends as well as co-workers but as I write this foreword I wonder why they asked me to do it. Many better-known missionaries or missiologists would have been happy to do it and thus given some 'name' recognition to the project.

But that is one of the points of this book. It is not the account of a superhero missionary. It is a chapter in God's Story that tells of various unlikely characters:

new missionaries struggling to overcome cultural and language barriers, witch doctors, illiterate women...

Another theme runs through this chapter: sacrifice. While Ronaldo talks about many sacrifices, it is Christ's sacrifice for us that is the focus.

Enjoy the Story. See it from a witch doctor's eyes. See how God is building His church. Marvel at His grace. Notice the kinds of people He uses. But don't stop there. Consider what kind of person you are!

When Moses asked, 'Who am I that I should go?' God replied, 'I will go with you,'—a subtle reminder that this Story of redemption is His Story. He then added His exclamation mark when He told Moses His name, 'I AM THAT I AM'.

God uses all who answer His call, including those who seem unlikely candidates. He uses anyone who knows that 'God is God', and that He is building His church.

As you read this story reflect on God's Story of redemption, who you are, and who God is. If you consider yourself an unlikely character to be involved in this—all the better. Listen for His call and write the chapter He has for you in His great Story.

Conrad Dueck

Acknowledgements

I am thankful to all the WEC team in Ghana for their friendship and care, especially our various field leaders since 1993: PM and Wabangla John, Jeanette Zwart and Anne Heath, for their encouragement and guidance. I am also grateful to the national and regional leaders of the Evangelical Church of Ghana who blessed us with their lives and teaching.

As we turn our thoughts to the Konkomba tribes in the north of Ghana, there are some people who deserve special mention.

Mary Steele, working with Wycliffe Bible Translators, initiated the translation of the New Testament into the Lichabol language, spoken by the Bichabol Konkombas of the Saboba Region, and later helped with the translation of the Old Testament. In partnership with Margaret Langdon, she also set up an adult education project in the mother tongue which became the point of reference for many new ministries including ours. When we arrived in Ghana in 1993, we had the privilege of meeting this aged and gracious lady who mirrored the person of Christ. Through her we were challenged to pray for the Bimonkpeln Konkombas with whom we eventually started working.

Praise God for Mary who, in the face of unimaginable restrictions and tribal wars, refused to abandon the work that God had entrusted to her!

In the late 1970s, Jan and Immy De Jong, working with WEC in partnership with the Evangelical Church of Ghana (ECG), used Mary Steele's Lichabol Bible material as a basis for a training programme for local Christians. Jan and Immy's vision for training leaders emphasized that people were more important than projects, and inspired many other workers including Dave and Sue Frampton.

David and Sue played an important role, not only in the whole missionary scenario, but also in our own lives. In the 1980s this lovely couple invested time, money and much energy in the training of leaders in various regions.

On our arrival, Dave introduced us to various parts of Ghana and showed us its needs. Most important of all, he gave us the vision for a broad-based ministry that would meet major spiritual and socials needs: the gospel, health, education and water.

The Framptons demonstrated the true meaning of self-denial so it is not surprising that when they left Ghana they also left behind a host of friends and admirers.

In 1998 Conrad and Brenda Dueck joined us in the work among the Konkombas and quickly became good friends. They captured our admiration, both for their undeniable dedication to the cause of Jesus and for their gift for training leaders, which had been one of our most obvious weaknesses.

The friendship of the Konkombas was a gift from the Lord. Our dear friends, Labuer Nimbu and Moses Makanda, were co-authors of this book. I am grateful for their help in correcting text, remembering extra details and contributing stories.

I would like to mention three people who helped at a later stage. Bob Harvey encouraged me to work on this book and then kindly translated it from Portuguese into English. (Through him I was challenged to join WEC in 1992 and I have been deeply blessed by his life and character through the years.) Jean Goodenough and Daphne Spraggett worked hard on the text, going through it several times, rearranging it and making great suggestions. Many thanks for your patience and kindness.

These precious people have, in different ways, helped us to walk with the Lord and to trust Him. I praise the Lord for all of them.

I must mention one more person. Revd Frans Leonard Schalkwijk was the Principal of the Presbyterian Seminary of the North (of Brazil). At the beginning of my course there, he challenged me, 'Do you want to be a missionary among people unreached with the gospel?' After hearing my timid response, he gave me some precious advice. One thing stuck in my mind, 'Study your Greek well, and it will save you years of work in Bible translation!'

Introduction

The Konkombas inhabit the north-east of Ghana and the north-west of Togo(see page 16). They constitute a nation of tribes that speak five major dialects, each with its own ethno-cultural distinctives. Each of these can, in turn, be subdivided into smaller dialects. The most well-known Konkomba tribes are the Bichabol, Bimonkpeln and the so-called Kombas.

Rossana and I went to Ghana in 1993 with WEC, having been sent out in partnership with the Agency for Cross-cultural Missions of the Brazilian Presbyterian Church. We sensed God leading us to locate in the Koni area and work among the Bimonkpeln, especially the Sanbol and Binalii clans who live in a vast region where the gospel had still not penetrated.

We devoted the first few months to learning the language and the culture. For some time we struggled to adapt ourselves to living with people whose week has only six days rather than seven, in a society where there are no years or ages.

Later, we experienced the problems that afflict new churches that develop in an animistic culture which has focused on the spirit world and the power of fetishes for millennia and where witch doctors are more powerful than the tribal chiefs. We had confrontations with polygamy, which society considers a virtue, and we faced the tremendous fragility of marriages based on the common practice of swapping sisters.

In addition, the vast number of languages spoken in the region made church services and worship more complicated.

However, after sixteen months, we had a small group of twelve converts. Then we had the privilege of witnessing a thrilling outpouring of the Holy Spirit. Through the grace of God, many Konkombas became believers, seventeen churches were planted, well-known fetish villages were reached and even witch doctors were converted.

God gave Rossana the vision of setting up a clinic that became a focal point in the whole region and we began a school that brought together children from various tribes and languages. We also developed a training programme for the eighty-one leaders who headed the churches planted over these years. The growth of the church in the Koni region made an impact on the culture, restricted the activity of witch doctors and transformed the tribal society along gospel lines.

The Konkomba church has sent evangelists into new areas, convincing me that before time began the Lord called the Konkombas to be a blessing to many peoples.

Following the advice of other workers in Ghana, I've changed the names of a few people, particularly those involved in illegal activities such as human sacrifice.

As you read this story, I pray that God will bless your own life through the testimony of this church in Ghana which, in the face of immense barriers, insists on believing that God will bring to pass in us everything that He has promised.

Explanation

The prefixes 'li-' and 'bi-' indicate number: 'li-' is singular as in Limonkpeln New Testament, and 'bi-' is plural as in Bimonkpeln people.

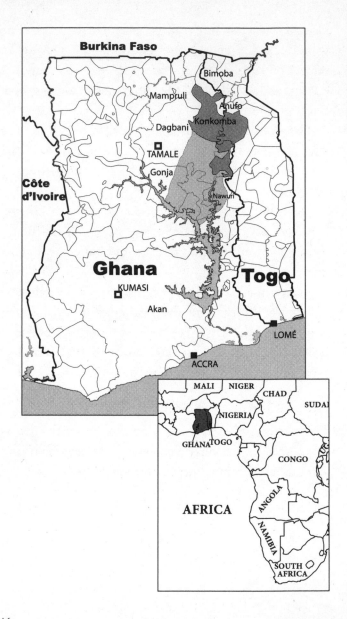

16

1969: MEBÁ
BRINGS GRUMADII

1

Mebá walked slowly through the dry savanna as the scorching sun cracked open the earth and compelled even the wind to be still. He had been making his way south for four days, fleeing the drought in the north and searching for fertile soil in which to grow yams. Trailing silently behind him were his wife Nadjo, four older children, three daughters-in-law and two grandchildren. Mebá carried his youngest son, Makanda, on his shoulders. Their destination was Koni, a remote village on the banks of the Molan River.

It was unusual for a man of Mebá's status to have only one wife for he was a witch doctor, the guardian of the Sanbol clan's fetish Grumadii, and as such would be expected to be a polygamist. Mebá carried the fetish in a small leather bag slung carefully over his left shoulder. While every Konkomba clan worships a fetish, the Sanbol fetish is considered particularly powerful. Known as a warrior fetish ('he who kills' or 'he who requires death'), Grumadii is feared by all the other clans. This fear has made the Sanbol extremely influential in some areas.

Suddenly, three-year-old Makanda broke the silence. From his vantage point on his father's shoulders, he had spotted an animal ahead of them.

'What's that?'

'A hyena,' answered Mebá, instinctively squeezing the bow that he kept ready in his left hand for any encounters with enemies or wild animals. At the mention of hyenas the whole group stepped up its pace. No one said a word but all wanted to find an inhabited place before dusk. A night-time confrontation with hyenas was something to be feared. Hunting in packs of up to sixty animals, they posed a serious threat to unprotected individuals or small groups. Mebá had just eight arrows in the quiver tied to his waist.

When they finally crossed a creek (which would later be named Nakpalbe, meaning 'a good place to stay') and heard voices in the distance, everyone breathed a sigh of relief. However, they had to sleep in the forest because night had already fallen and Mebá had not had time to sacrifice to his fetish. Without that sacrifice no Grumadii witch doctor was allowed to enter a new village.

Next morning, Mebá sacrificed a goat and poured its blood over the exposed roots of a large tree. Having left their homeland, these followers of Grumadii needed to ensure that distant spirits would come and transport the sacrifice to the land they had left, and would normally seek out a site at a crossroads close to the village that would become their new home. Having done all that was necessary to satisfy the fetish, the family could at last go into the village.

Situated in virgin forest and at that time home to 200 villagers, Koni is surrounded by tall, leafy trees. Neatly-thatched round huts are erected in a circle for greater protection, and grouped into three distinct areas each belonging to a different tribe.

When Mebá walked into Koni with his family, the villagers immediately identified him as a member of the Sanbol clan by his facial markings and dialect, so Laason, the oldest man of that clan, welcomed him. That night, as the Sanbols took Mebá round to the huts of the other clans, they announced, 'Grumadii has arrived!'

A special ceremony marked the coming of Grumadii to Koni and several trees on the edge of Koni were designated as a sacred place. Sankan, the local witch doctor, knew a sacrifice would be required. When he took the small white stones used to call up spirits and invoked Grumadii, the spirit responded by taking possession of Sankan's wife, whose body was overcome with spasms.

'What sacrifice does my lord desire?' asked Sankan.

'In order for me to look after you alone, separate twelve animals for me,' croaked the spirit in a quiet voice. 'If you want me to look after *all* of you, separate a child.'

There were various views about how Grumadii expressed his anger if a sacrifice was denied him, but all focused on natural calamities, epidemics and sudden deaths. Strangely, one proverb said that Grumadii never *asked* for a sacrifice, but merely *suggested* one.

Sankan sat down, bowing his head, as he pondered the implications of the spirit's instructions. He took great satisfaction in knowing that Grumadii had spoken on his compound and now he began to work out which member of his family it would be most appropriate to sacrifice. Konkombas normally chose younger children, especially if they were sick, because they might die anyway. At least, that is what one Binaliib proverb recommended! Sankan's decision was made easier when he heard that Una, his eight-month-old grandson, was coughing and burning up with fever. Una was the first-born son of Kofu and Ado.

'We will pacify Grumadii's anger with Kofu's son!'

When she heard of Sankan's choice, Ado knew she had only two options: to flee or remain silent. She looked at Kofu with a mixture of sadness and bitterness but said nothing. That night Sankan took the sick baby from his mother's arms. A few hours later the child was placed on a rock and killed with one blow from a club. Before burning their 'offering' to Grumadii, the people danced round and round the battered corpse.

Sankan was happy in the days that followed. This act inaugurated the era of Grumadii at Koni, which became a fetish centre for the region. As for Ado, she was given puna, the most delicious of yams, for six days as a recompense for the sacrifice of her child.

No one could publicly mourn Una's death and his name was now taboo, never to be mentioned again. In the Konkomba culture, the living, the dead, the absent and the sick are identified by titles and occupy different levels on the social ladder. Those chosen for sacrifice receive no title whatsoever and are deleted from the family history as if they had never existed.

Other events accompanied the coming of Grumadii to Koni. Collective demon possession characterised Nnupan, the festival of new yams. During Namise, the festival of fire, sacrifices were offered to the earth. The village grew as more and more people moved to the region to gain the protection of the fetish.

Because Mebá was so well acquainted with the Grumadii ceremonies, people began to call him the Guardian of the Dwarf and referred to him as the Friend of Grumadii when performing ceremonies for other fetishes. Dwarves were reputed to have the ability to forecast the future and explain the present. The mystic title of Guardian was reserved for those who not only understood the technicalities of the ceremonies linked to a specific fetish, but had also established a personal relationship with the spirits that guided it.

From 1969 to 1994, Grumadii reigned supreme, and because Mebá was greatly respected he was given good land and had many people working for him.

During those years, little happened to alter the way that Konkombas viewed the world. To be born into Konkomba society meant following a set of rituals and ceremonies that were an integral part of tribal life and survival. There was no distinction between sacred and secular, spiritual and material, or body and soul. The 'religious' was present in every expression of life: work, food, wars, procreation and rest. Atheists were non-existent. Everybody believed in the spirit world and in the fetishes (mountains, trees, rocks and even man-made objects) that represented the various spirits. They also believed in totems: animals or birds that were sacred to the clan. Often there were stories to explain the special relationship with the totem.

Perhaps it had helped to rescue them in the past or it may have a characteristic, such as courage, strength or wisdom, with which the clan wanted to identify.

One of the spirits in which they believed was Kininbon (Satan), lord of all the evil spirits. The spirits also included the souls of the ancestors who demanded respect and sacrifices in return for withholding punishment.

There were no good spirits—the best were merely amoral.

Parallel to that vast universe of wickedness, everyone had heard about Uwumbor, an ancient God of a bygone era and distant dreams, who no longer had any relationship with the tribe. Uwumbor was the creator of everything: heaven and earth, and the first family. At first he was very close to earth but then, according to the Konkombas, 'One of our ancestors committed a wicked deed and because of that offence Uwumbor no longer wishes to be God of the Konkombas.' The details of that terrible crime have long since been forgotten, but because of it Uwumbor went far away and took heaven with him. There was no way back to meet Uwumbor any more, so the people had to seek other ways of minimising the suffering caused by his absence.

1994: News of Uwumbor

During the next twenty-five years, the Konkomba view of the world remained unchanged. Then, in December 1994, Koni received another visitor— a white man who came with news of Uwumbor. Some months earlier, our field leader, P.M. John, had given me the green light to start surveying the villages of the north-eastern region of Ghana, mapping their clans and languages. So, for the last four months I had been conducting the survey while Rossana remained in Accra with our newborn daughter, Vivianne.

I still remember my arrival in that remote village whose name means, 'Come! Enter!' At the end of the trail, a river and three creeks border Koni. As I approached a thicket of large trees in my search for the village, a flock of beautiful white birds suddenly flew off towards another three tall trees which stood leafy and straight some distance away. Going in that direction, I saw the first huts of Koni. It appeared to be a beautiful place.

The arrival of a white man caused a stir in the village. Young children ran away in fear but some of the older ones risked stroking my arm, wondering if white skin felt different from black skin. It did not take long for some of them to give me the nickname Likoldubil (peeled banana)! Once they had overcome their initial shock at seeing a white person, the people proved to be friendly and hospitable. However, right up to the time we left, some years later, we still heard mothers threatening their children, 'If you do that, the white man will get you!'

The chief's brother invited me to stay in his house. As it would be several months before Rossana arrived, I settled down to learn one of the Limonkpeln dialects, and become familiar with the local culture. Although I had previously lived in Nakpai, another Konkomba village, its people belonged to a different clan whose culture was different from that of the people in Koni.

The official welcome to the newly-arrived ukalja (white man) gave me my first chance to preach the gospel. The ceremony was held near the chief's house in the shade of three huge trees. Because it was Mandjaa, the last day of the six-day Konkomba week, it was also a rest day so almost everyone in Koni came along for the occasion.

After the initial formalities, one of the village elders stood up.

'We call you Ukalja but I know you must have a name.' He was about to ask the question I had been eagerly anticipating.

'What is your name?'

I still remember the stir my answer caused.

'The Konkombas call me Uwumbor Bi!' While some people merely repeated my name, others laughed or shook their heads in disbelief. The village elders, in particular, could not understand how a white man could have a Konkomba name—especially one so full of meaning.

I had been given the name by the Konkombas of Nakpai village. Rossana and I had arrived in Ghana in September 1993 and, after two months of prayer and research, were sent to this village where fellow WECers Dave and Sue Frampton had lived and started a church. The villagers appeared happy and hospitable and were proud that more people from a distant country had come to live among them!

Despite the welcome, the first three weeks were hard for us. Faced with a new culture, not to mention a language that has twenty-three distinct secondary dialects, we felt lost. We struggled to adapt to living in a place where the people use a six-day week, where there are no years or ages, and where polygamy is considered a virtue.

We knew we needed to study the language, to understand the culture and compare it with the Word of God, and to discover ways of expounding the Word; but we were to learn that it was Jesus Himself—not us—who was building His church.

Like Sue Frampton before her, Rossana helped those who were sick. Although only a nurse, she found herself treating all kinds of diseases ranging from skin conditions and inflammation of the gums to malaria, hepatitis, tuberculosis and meningitis. Her patients, who came in from surrounding villages and from Nakpai itself, expected to be given a litapalpel (literally 'white stone'), a term which originally alluded to the white chloroquine tablets used to combat malaria, and that generally came to mean any medication.

One sunny morning, typical of the days preceding the Harmattan season when the wind blows down from the Sahara, Rossana got her medicines ready as usual, and laid out disposable gloves along with a supply of cotton wool and sticking plaster. I went outside to greet several elderly patients who were waiting under a nearby tree. That day we attended to twenty or so patients, helping them as much as we could within our limitations. By eleven o'clock everyone had been seen, so we sat down to rest under the big tree in front of our house.

A woman approached carrying a baby. She was obviously not a Konkomba, having the paler skin and finer features of one of the northern peoples. In addition, she held her child in her arms, unlike Konkombas who tie babies on their backs with a large cloth. When she spoke she used a language we did not know, so we sought help from some villagers who knew Dagbani and Hausa, common northern languages.

'I belong to the Fulani-Krê people,' explained the woman, 'and I have come because I heard that once again there are some white people here who are healing those who are sick.' (The Fulani-Krê are nomadic Fulas from the south of Burkina Faso. A small ethnic group, they are strongly influenced by Islam and very opposed to the gospel.)

'May I look at your baby?' Rossana asked.

The woman handed over the little girl and Rossana took her in her arms.

The seven-month-old child was a horrible sight, covered from head to foot in ugly growths. One big tumour near her left ear made her head look deformed. Yellow pus oozed from cracks in the tumours, soaking the cloth in which she was wrapped. The child's eyes were inflamed, she had a fever—certainly due to the infection—and was having difficulty breathing. Even her crying was almost inaudible.

'It started about three months ago,' explained the mother. 'Almost every day the skin cracked and another wound appeared. The Fulani medicine men don't know what to do.' The woman looked tired and dejected, worn out by sleepless nights worrying about her daughter and by the long walk to get to Nakpai.

Rossana and I looked at each other. Our small supply of medicines was almost finished and we knew there was no way we could adequately treat the child there and then.

'Usually we have medicine which can help to cure the more common diseases like malaria,' said Rossana, 'but at the moment we don't have what we need to treat your little girl.'

The mother bowed her head despondently, but Rossana continued, 'However, we know something which is not a pill but is more powerful than any medicine. If you so desire, it can heal your daughter.'

The woman looked up.

'What is it?'

'There is a God, whom we serve. He is the only God, and has power over everything, even the body, the earth and the spirits!'

Through our interpreter, we explained who God is. The woman listened attentively as we told her about His love and about Yesu Kristu, His Son, and the salvation promised to all peoples, including the Fulani-Krê. Finally we said, 'We can ask this God to heal your daughter with His power.'

Then we prayed, giving time for each sentence to be translated into her language.

'Do you believe?' asked Rossana.

Serenely she replied, 'I believe.'

We then did our best to clean the child's sores using mercurochrome diluted with a little water to make it go further, and then wrapped her in a new, clean cloth. After we had done all we could, the woman stood up and left.

During the next four days we were so immersed in our language study that we forgot all about the Fulani-Krê woman and her daughter. Then, late one afternoon, we once more saw the tall, slim figure approaching. I must confess that I had butterflies in my stomach as she got closer and I could see that she held a motionless child wrapped in a cloth. My immediate thought was that the child had died, but the mother's expression was strange. As she stopped in front of us she broke into a huge smile which transformed her face, and unwrapped the cloth to reveal the child—fast asleep! I hoped the child would be much improved with tumours that were shrinking. But I was stunned by what I saw. The tumours had disappeared! In awe, we ran our hands over the baby's chest and the head that had been so deformed by the huge tumours.

Now there was nothing, absolutely nothing: no sores, no pus—not even a scar! The only evidence of her dreadful illness was old skin peeling off.

'God has heard!' exclaimed the mother between smiles.

Then an unforgettable scene, like none I had ever witnessed before, unfolded before us. The woman started going from hut to hut showing her child to everyone in that Konkomba village and telling them about Uwumbor, the God who saves! God had called us to take the gospel to this tribe but now we began to understand that, regardless of any feeble missionary efforts, it is Jesus Himself who builds His Church throughout the earth. Hallelujah! The woman's testimony made an impact on many people and they began to seek us out.

Then came the event that would later produce such surprise among the Konkombas of Koni village. It started when a few elders from a neighbouring village admitted that they had a certain difficulty with us.

'We are delighted that you are living among us,' they said, 'and the people in the other villages are also happy to have you here, but we do have one problem.'

We were puzzled.

'What is it?'

'Your names! They are appalling and we can't get our tongues round them. We can't imagine how your parents could have given you such strange names!'

So we asked them whether it would be possible for them to give us Konkomba names.

Up to that point we were seeing it as a kind of cultural joke, little realising that the Holy Spirit was preparing a remarkable strategy for reaching those people. The dialect spoken by the Konkombas in Nakpai is a proverbial language. This means that children's names reflect particular events surrounding the time of their birth. Just as in the Old Testament, names are chosen for their meaning rather than for the way they sound, so among the Konkombas there are names like Jagri (the one who left but came back), Unidanyun (if you have a family you will be well known), or Usaan Nyan (the path is a very good one).

Several days later, the elders summoned us to tell us our new names. They looked at Rossana and said, 'We wish to call her Dotapii—the woman who heals.' In this way they acknowledged Rossana's role as the one who treated the sick people.

'And you will no longer be called Ronaldo, but Uwumbor Bi—the one who says, "There is a God!"'

Here was the Holy Spirit bringing to birth, in the language of the people, a way to proclaim the gospel. Wherever we went we were always asked, 'What are your names?'

From that day forward, I could reply, 'My name is Uwumbor Bi—the one who says, "There is a God!"' Immediately, the people would raise their eyebrows

33

and ask, 'But who is this God?' And we would answer, 'Go to your huts and make a campfire. Tonight we will sit round it with you and explain who this God is.'

And so it was that in Koni, as elsewhere, my new name provided opportunities for talking about the God who is there. We were encouraged by the knowledge that the healing of the child and our new names were both evidence of the Holy Spirit in action. It showed us that the Lord is in a hurry to reach every unreached tribe. God blessed us with a definite conviction that from before time began He had determined to extend His hand and touch the Konkomba tribe in this area with His grace.

The Holy Spirit began to unsettle many people's hearts, and they came from near and far asking, 'Is what we hear true? Is there a new arrival in Koni who knows about Uwumbor, and bears His name?'

'Mantotiib' Between God and Man

Every missionary who seeks to evangelise an unreached people group must face the question: 'How much of the gospel does this person (or group) need to hear for the Spirit to produce genuine repentance in them and bring them to salvation?'

Because the theoretical concept of salvation meant little to the Konkombas we had to use an approach which considered their history, culture and beliefs. We knew, for instance, that stories and words of people 'who lived before' carried the weight of truth. In the culture of an animistic society, ancestors have a pivotal role in terms of values, history and knowledge of the spiritual world.

For example, while we may say that the story of Adam talks about 'creation and the fall', in proverbial-ancestor language it tells about 'a man who was near to God, but abandoned his home'. In the Konkomba culture they often speak about 'an ancestor of all who know God'. When this ancestor is identified as Abraham, it helps the Konkombas to see that they, too, are part of God's plan.

The prophets who 'sang' the promise of the Messiah are perceived as 'those who saw Him who would come, and spoke about Him'.

We needed to be particularly careful when referring to Jesus, so we delayed talking about Him until we had gained a greater understanding of the Konkomba culture. We were a little afraid of referring to Him as Uwumbor Aabu ('He who is the Son of God') because the expression Son of God could have several different meanings. It could, for example, refer to a man when he was installed as a local chief. Children could be called Uwumbor Aabu when offered as sacrifices. Even certain types of strong fetishes were called Uwumbor Aabu when they displayed unusual power to call up rain, heal the sick or drive away enemies.

Although a Konkomba Bible existed in the Lichabol dialect we now realised that the Limonkpeln dialect would need a separate translation. We began translating the Gospel of Matthew and used it to teach the people who Jesus is. It was then that we suddenly stumbled on a great cultural treasure—the Mantotiib.

The Mantotiib, which is still practised among Konkombas, is a special sacrifice used to heal a broken relationship: for example when enmity has developed between two men or where a disagreement in a family has led one member to isolate himself from the rest. Originally Mantotiib simply meant 'joint sacrifice' but because of the way it has been used in the community for the practical outworking of reconciliation, it has acquired the meaning 'sacrifice for forgiveness'.

The Mantotiib gave us our first opportunity to explain, in a culturally acceptable way, who Jesus is and why He came to live among us. Our explanation went like this:

'God entered into Manotiib with people so they could once again have a way of access to the Creator. But, just as the animal sacrifices used in the Manotiib are powerless to avoid a future break in relationships, so the sacrifices of the Old Testament were unable to reunite us with God permanently.'

Then we announced the good news!

> But there was Jesus,
> who was handed over as a sacrifice of reconciliation
> between God and people
> so that every person would be able,
> like Adam,
> to see God once again.

Although the application of this cultural analogy seemed reasonable to us, the Konkomba were puzzled.

'How did all this happen without our knowing about it?' some asked. Others wondered, 'How could people continue to reject God after He had decided to establish an agreement with them?'

As they struggled to relate this teaching to their tribal worldview it became obvious that the wisest thing would be to give them time to discuss the message and decipher it culturally. We decided not to try to introduce new points too quickly and for a whole week added nothing to what we had already shared. We wandered around chatting with individuals or small groups wherever they were. We visited them at home, talked with them as they rested under the trees, accompanied them to their fields or stopped to chat with women on their way to the river.

We soon learnt that Konkomba has no words for 'grace' or 'salvation' so we tried to explain the concepts using long-winded proverbs. However, these did not always communicate the exact meanings as expressed in the Word of God. We realised we needed to spend much more time researching the culture in order to express these ideas in a way that was accurate and intelligible.

After two weeks of these informal discussions, we decided to go into greater detail about the person of Jesus and His origin using Matthew's Gospel because of its focus on Christ's genealogy. The Konkombas asked questions that were difficult to answer at the time!

'If Jesus rose from the dead, doesn't that mean that God annulled His Mantotiib?'

'Jesus wouldn't be an incorporated spirit, would he?' (An incorporated spirit is one that can use different bodies to appear before men.)

'Is Jesus one of our ancestors?'

'Was Jesus a "total man"?'

Answers to questions about ancestors were difficult to formulate because the Konkombas' ideas of 'ancestors' were restrictive and had serious social implications. To become an ancestor, a man must have had at least two wives, fathered many children and lived a reasonably long life! As for being a 'total man' this was impossible for any man who had never married. Such a person is considered to be a child even when he is very old!

We continued our evening discussions, sitting with villagers in their huts or under trees.

By this time we had translated portions from seventeen chapters of Matthew's Gospel and our teaching focused on 'Jesus Christ, complete Man, Son of God, Lord and Bridge of reconciliation.'

The Konkombas were already familiar with the idea of faith and forgiveness. It was common knowledge that 'a man will never carry a fetish unless he believes in its power', and that 'you never forget what has never been forgiven'. Consequently it was easy to communicate these central elements of the gospel and we gave great emphasis to them. We were aware, however, that genuine repentance is the core issue for measuring any movement of God and we were still waiting for that to become evident among the people of Koni.

Without doubt the communication of the gospel is totally linked to culture. So, while we were learning more of the language and culture of the people, the Holy Sprit was working at what He has always been doing since time began—bringing genuine repentance to birth in the hearts of people.

By April 1995 we had visited all the huts in Koni, talking about God and the Messiah who is promised to all peoples. This was in preparation for preaching the full gospel. Already the Konkombas were referring to Jesus as the Mantotiib of God and there existed a strong feeling both on our part and the tribe's that something momentous was going to happen. We had spoken about the action of the Holy Spirit who would transform lives; yet in reality their understanding was still vague.

REBIRTH OF A WITCH DOCTOR

All the time that this was going on, one person stayed in the background.

We had little personal contact with Mebá, because of the nature of a witch doctor's life. We knew him only as a witch doctor who had been feared by the people since he arrived in Koni. We also knew there were nights when he was involved in sacrificing up to 300 animals to Grumadii and other fetishes. Yet, he was not openly opposed to the gospel and even allowed us into his compound to share the Word of God with his family. Twice he had listened to what we had to say.

One rest day as I was taking a shower, a young fellow came running up shouting, 'Something is happening to Mebá!' I dressed quickly and joined a small crowd of curious villagers that had quickly gathered at the witch doctor's hut on the edge of the village. Normally a talkative man, Mebá had been very quiet that day and had sat in the shade of a tree deep in thought.

But now he was excited: jumping, dancing and yelling!

'Mebá, what's happening?' someone asked.

He responded joyfully, 'There is something new inside me. I began to think about what they are saying about Yesu Kristu, and suddenly understanding came to me. I had been afraid of Grumadii's wrath and its consequences, but now I know that Yesu Kristu is truly the Son of God! What I have understood today is that Yesu Kristu, God among us, is more powerful than Grumadii! There is nothing to fear!'

There and then he was converted: he had been born again and was fascinated by it all. For two whole days he was wide-awake, singing and testifying excitedly about the Lord. When speaking about the gospel he was insistent and challenging. He couldn't even sit down! From the first day people started saying, 'If you go to Mebá's home, sleep or even eat there, the Spirit of the Christians will enter you!'

He brought all his fetishes, jujus and idols to the first meeting after his conversion and together we burned them. That day, immediately following the beautiful, impacting testimony of his conversion, I preached on the vast number of human gods and the one divine God of Psalm 115.

Not surprisingly, the village reacted with shock to the news of the Grumadii witch doctor's conversion. The event was so serious and made such an impact that the village chief hurriedly called an Elders' Council. We never discovered what was decided at their meeting, but we do know that Mebá's entire family were immediately persecuted. Not only did they lose privileges in the Elder's Council but at least two attempts were made to poison them.

Mebá's seven sons and two daughters all accepted the Lord and became leading members of the Koni church. I remember the contagious joy that overwhelmed Mebá during the morning service in which his wife, with tears in her eyes, finally surrendered herself to the Lord.

It is a Konkomba custom to sing when there is a special reason for thanksgiving. After her conversion Nadjo sang this song:

> When you come to Jesus,
>   you will see what life is,
> The sun will shine brighter for you,
> The trees will be greener for you,
> Everything in your life will change.

Today Mebá is the oldest of the elders of the ten Konkomba churches in the Koni area. As a close friend, I can bear witness that he is a man of God, filled with the Holy Spirit, and an inspiration to us every time we meet him. Praise be to God who changes hearts!

Meba's son, Makanda, was already known in the village for his humility and dedication. A brilliant young man, he spoke at least ten dialects, and helped Rossana by interpreting for the sick people who came to our house for treatment. We saw his potential immediately and encouraged him to study nursing. He followed our advice and qualified as a Health Assistant. After the construction of the clinic in Koni, he became head of staff as well as being responsible for the medical ministry.

One day, he told us his story.

'Before we were Christians we worshipped a fetish called Babasu which was located in the village of Sibru. We believed it could either heal and protect us, or kill us. I was fascinated by its power. Once I travelled to Sibru to work in the fields of the local witch doctor (a man who was well known in the region and feared by all) until the day of the sacrifice.

'There were various kinds of sacrifices, but on that morning he was going to sacrifice chickens. They were killed with a blow and we watched how they fell to the ground. When it came to my turn the chicken fell with its legs downwards which meant the fetish had rejected the sacrifice. I tried again and again until my sacrifice was accepted. Then the blood was poured over a foul-smelling fetish altar: a small stone table, black with blood. Afterwards, the witch doctor gave me a specially prepared nut as a sign that the fetish had accepted me and I was now under its protection.

'When I returned to Koni I continued to seek the fetish by sharing in the sacrifices, and I made the name of Babasu well known. I also started to drink a lot. One day, which I remember well even though I was drunk, a white man suddenly appeared in Koni. What a day that was! Children were crying and everyone was curious to see the white man up close.

'The weeks rolled by and the white man kept coming. Some time later he told us about a God who is greater than our fetishes. This message stirred up everyone especially the witch doctors who soon began to accuse him of being a liar. But something kept telling me that what he said could be the truth. It compelled me to listen over and over again. I heard about the power of God (the white man's favourite theme) and about salvation through Jesus. One day he spoke to us about the Holy Spirit.

'I can't explain all that happened nor the precise day that I began to believe in God, but at some point I saw the light of Jesus near, and a sense of freedom took hold of my life. From that day on I could sum up my experience with God in a song which says,

> Before I did not know where Jesus was,
> And I was looking for ways of salvation.
> When you see Jesus, you see the light.

'Without doubt my father's experience also made a great impression on me. The transformation in his life was so radical that something real had to be happening. Jesus was not just "a white man's fable" as some were saying.'

Makanda, now a church leader, says, 'When someone asks me what is so precious about Jesus, I love to answer, "When you see Jesus, you see the light."'

A Church Is Born

5

Mebá was one of thirteen converts who were the first-fruits of the slowly advancing work. As well as pre-evangelising various Konkomba clans we also contacted the Chokosis and Fulanis, ethnic minorities living on the outskirts of the village. Traditionally, the Konkombas allowed these foreigners to cultivate their land on condition that they showed their respect for the Konkomba by learning their language and dances. From their first days in the village, the Chokosis and Fulanis restricted the use of their mother tongue and customs to the privacy of their own huts.

Before our first open-air meeting in Koni, we went from hut to hut inviting everyone to join us. The appointed place was a leafy tree, which was well-known because a fetish was set up on one side of it. We met on the other side. About 120 people turned up. Many of them were simply curious observers but the rest were sent by the witch doctors.

For one and a half hours three drums beat out the rhythm of the first-ever Christian Konkomba music in Koni, leading the people in praise and worship in their own dialect. During the meeting God spoke so powerfully and showed His presence in such a way that the meeting made an enormous impact on the life of the Church in the Koni area.

After I taught from the Word of God, sixty-six Konkombas came forward and knelt down to hand their lives over to the Lord Jesus. We prayed for them and consecrated them. Then, with rejoicing, we announced the time of our next meeting.

But God had not finished! Glancing to the left, I noticed a crippled Chokosi woman. Now thirty-eight years old, she had contracted polio as a child. With legs as useless as jelly, she used her arms and hands to drag herself around. Until this point, we had not seen any openness to the gospel in her clan, although we had shared the good news with them. But the seed was about to spring into life in this woman, prompting her to leave her compound for the first time since contracting polio and drag herself to the tree where we were meeting. Crawling through the bush for two kilometres took a long time. She arrived covered in mud, with hair filthy from the dust and hands bleeding from sharp rocks. I remember her so well, stretched out on the ground, raising her right hand and asking, 'Is there a chance for *me* to accept the Lord Jesus, too?'

As we watched this woman cover her face with her hands, in the act of giving her life to the Lord Jesus, we saw a perfect picture of the birth of the Church among the people in our area. God was taking seriously His decision to reach not only the Konkombas but also the tribes that lived round them. Hallelujah!

The other villagers began to ask, 'What is happening to these people?'

To this question would come the answer, 'It's called Asori (Church). They are the followers of Jesus.'

Among the men who accepted the Lord at that first public meeting were two brothers, Nakpabu and Uwiin, members of the Binaliib clan which had founded the village. They began to share the gospel with their brother Kidiik and regularly asked prayer for him.

Now a slim young man, Kidiik had spent his time alone, perched on a rock or wandering through the jungle that surrounded the village. He had been chosen from birth as the future village Ubua—the guardian of the fetishes. (It is only through the sacrifice of animals or people that the fetishes can be invoked or 'touched', and the Ubua is responsible for the rituals

49

accompanying these sacrifices. He pours blood over the fetish to pacify the anger of the offended spirit, to secure his presence among them or to seek more spiritual power for some specific purpose.) The right of instructing an Ubua child is transferred from his family to the current Ubua. The child grows up in seclusion and is undisciplined. As a result, he becomes a loner, rarely speaking and avoiding any gatherings of people.

Kidiik's selection for this role was a result of his intense struggle for survival during the three days that his mother was in labour. He would have been just five years old when he started to learn the intricate system of rules and practices for the fetish ceremonies for which he would be responsible when he became the Ubua.

At around seven years old Kidiik had to submit to the first ritual of consecration during which his head was shaved and animals were sacrificed to the local fetish. From that moment on the elders began teaching him the names and functions of each spirit that inhabits the world. Each group of spirits demands different and regular ceremonies to prevent them from punishing the tribe and the village.

On reaching adolescence, the Ubua learns the names of his ancestors and how to invoke them; but only as an adult can he learn about the sacrifices. Throughout his life he must observe strict rules. He may never eat pork, monkey, antelope or birds; except for sacrifices, he should never look at a dead body; he has no rights to his children who should be brought up by one of his brothers; and at certain times of the year he is not to sit with people who are chatting together. As for his wife, she must always take a bath before preparing his food and is not allowed to cook for him at all during her monthly period.

Year by year Kidiik was meticulously trained in the art of sacrifice and fetish control. After some time it was said that there were only two people in the whole area who possessed 'total authority' from Grumadii: Njabi, the witch doctor and Kidiik, his apprentice. During that period Kidiik was able to exercise control over some minor fetishes, and on certain occasions, he could even make fetishes for other witch doctors. In the animistic world of fetishes, such a level of relationship between man and fetish is not a daily occurrence.

Recalling his experiences with the fetishes Kidiik said, 'I learned all the arts of spiritual control beginning with the power of certain fetishes. I started attacking people spiritually, even from great distances. I invoked the ancestors and conversed with them to discover secrets from the past. And I made sacrifices with the specific objectives of either helping people or making situations more complicated. I hadn't the slightest doubt about the existence and power of the gods and spirits that inhabit our world. However, once a witch doctor gets to know the spirits, he begins to see, more clearly than anyone, just how fallen they are. There is nothing good in their motives and objectives. Even when seeming to help one person it is generally to the detriment of another. Every experience ends in great sadness: separation, anger, fighting, deception, lying or death.'

After a time it was obvious that Kidiik was interested in the gospel and the effect that it was having on the new converts.

Njabi, who was responsible for Kidiik's training, also noticed his interest. He instructed some children to keep an eye on him to make sure that he kept his distance from both the followers of Christ and the growing number of people who gathered in little groups every day to discuss the gospel.

But Njabi could not stop the Holy Spirit working! One morning Kidiik was ploughing in his yam plantation when suddenly he sensed God was touching him in a profound way. Instantly, he abandoned his work and rushed back to the village where we were holding a meeting under a tree. He raced up to us and we waited for him to get his breath back. Overcome with emotion and with tears rolling down his face, he threw himself onto the ground and cried out, 'Yesu!' We formed a circle round him as he called on the Name of the Lord Jesus. While praying, he made a declaration that would later become one of the church's songs: 'Truly, I know that God is God!'

Kidiik became one of the most forthright witnesses in our region. Every time he gave his testimony he said the same thing, 'I used to be a witch doctor, but now I'm free.' After publicly speaking out about the secrets of occultism and the fetishes, he would proclaim Jesus to the people. One day he was walking to the village of Saiwontido with Labuer, another of the early Christians who would later train to take over as pastor of the Koni Church. People who had known Kidiik as a slave of the fetishes started shouting, 'Now Kidiik is free! Kidiik is free!' This gave Labuer the opening to put out the challenge, 'Wouldn't you like to be free, too?' As a result there were conversions in Saiwontido that day.

Like Mebá, Kidiik lost all his privileges in the village and with the elders because of becoming a Christian. Many of those who had knowledge of fetishism and had gone through similar apprenticeships began to persecute him. It affected his family, too. When Kidiik abandoned the fetishes his younger brother took his place as the guardian of one of them. Immediately, this young fellow was stung by a scorpion and was in terrible pain for three days.

Kidiik was among the first elders we appointed in 1996, along with Mebá, Makanda, Kofi and Labuer. The church in Koni was growing. Although Koni was by no means the largest of the forty-eight Konkomba villages in the area, its church set a standard for the others.

The Church on the Move

'Have you heard about Jesus?'

As the church grew, this became the standard question in Konkomba communities for miles around Koni. The gospel touched more and more villages because of the testimony of those who had come to the Lord in Koni. The Name of Jesus Christ was beginning to pass from mouth to mouth throughout the whole region.

After several months of teaching the new believers in Koni, we heard about a village called Molan, situated further north on the other side of the Molan River. A quick exploratory trip revealed that the Sanboln were the predominant clan in this area.

With its deep, turbulent water, the river proved to be a formidable obstacle when we tried to cross it. Despite rowing with all our might our small canoe, carved from a single tree trunk, made slow progress against the strong current. Drifting weeds and trees uprooted by the rains were extra hazards. After completing the crossing we quickly set out on foot towards Molan and arrived at the village, which consisted of about thirty compounds, without incident.

The villagers were hospitable. They provided a meal of yam chunks served with a freshly cooked bush rat, the Konkombas' way of giving us a warm welcome. Traditionally, one of the young men goes off to hunt for a bush rat or similar small game, kill it and bring it to the visitor. The latter remains seated and accepts the creature with both hands. He carefully inspects it, turning it from side to side, and finally squeezes it until blood oozes from the eyes or ears. This is proof that the meat is fresh. The visitor exclaims, 'Hummmm!' (Appetising!), which is the signal for the oldest lady in the household to take the meat and hurry off to prepare it. Thirty minutes later, the meal is ready and everyone stands around watching the visitor attentively as he, alone, tries the food. When he moves his head from side to side this is a positive sign that the meal is delicious.

We visited Molan five times explaining the gospel to individuals and families before holding our first meeting at which more than twenty adults came to the Lord. One of them, Gbaba, caught our attention. A tall, thin young man, he had a powerful voice and spoke with eloquence. He soon showed himself to be a leader. Anxious to learn the Word of God, he crossed the river every week and walked to Koni to learn the verses the new converts there were memorising. When we started a reading programme in Limonkpeln, the mother tongue of Koni, Gbaba was one of the first people in his village to learn to read. Having learnt so quickly, he made photocopies of the texts that we had already translated and used them to teach the gospel, in detail, to believers and unbelievers in his village. Six months later, the church at Molan had grown so much that they were able to help us plant a church in another village, Jimoni, where we had began a pre-evangelisation process.

One thing that intrigued me was the way that everyone on the northern side of the river accepted Gbaba as leader of the churches. For 500 years the Konkombas had enslaved people from smaller or weaker tribes. Although no longer slaves, and their descendants are Konkomba in culture and language, they are treated as second-class citizens and not normally accepted as leaders. Gbaba's family fell into this category, which made it surprising that he could be recognised as a leader by the entire church in Molan and Jimoni. Their acceptance of him was a vivid demonstration of 'gospel culture' and contributed tremendously to our ability to teach the Christians in Koni, Molan and Jimon about their spiritual heritage. In turn, this understanding helped the church to gel together.

The whole tribe soon realised that the fellowship between believers was something special. They could see the way they worked together, helped each other and shared their joys and sorrows. As the news about the church of Christ spread, we found people waiting for the gospel to come to their village so they could respond to it! This was the way the villages of Sibru and Sakoni were reached.

Not everything was so easy or straightforward. The enemy counter-attacked and local witch doctors fanned hatred in the hearts of the unbelievers. The shrapnel of hatred, persecution and indifference wounded many believers.

As the church grew, Rossana and I were persecuted, too. Our opponents prohibited our entering some villages. They tried to oppress us with fetish music, dancing and singing round our house. On several occasions we received death threats and in December 1997 an attempt was made to kill us by poisoning our water. This resulted in serious illness for the whole family, particularly Junior who was only one year old at the time. However, the Lord's constant protection ensured that the witness of the gospel not only continued but also grew.

In April 1997 God challenged the churches of Molan and Jimoni to reach out to the village of Kadjokora in the extreme north. Together with local church leaders, I went on three trips through the region pre-evangelising the village's five clans. We met strong resistance from two witch doctors who constantly screamed insults and curses at us. Nevertheless, after six weeks we prepared for the first public meeting. The day before it was due to be held, a storm hit the whole region. The bad weather took us by surprise but we decided against cancelling the meeting.

Mebá decided to go with me, riding pillion on my motorbike. (The bike made the river crossing even trickier because we had to keep it upright in the canoe!) The church leaders from Molan and Jimoni joined with us on the way to Kadjokora. On our arrival, we saw that the people were ready despite the bad weather. We held the meeting under a huge tree during a break in the rain. We began with a time of praise then Mebá gave a powerful testimony, challenging everyone to follow Jesus 'the most powerful One of all'. At this point the group became uneasy and the village chief began pacing backwards and forwards. We saw the village elders and two witch doctors approach him, possibly intending to get him to boycott the rest of the meeting. After the message, we invited people to come to the Lord Jesus. This provoked an immediate reaction in the witch doctors. Standing behind me, they hurled threats at anyone who was considering surrendering to Christ. 'Those who follow this Yesu will certainly die in a few days,' they screamed.

As the tension mounted, Giba (a Christian from the Molan Church) began to sing. The words of the song he chose were very appropriate:

> If anyone tells you they know another way,
> don't believe them
> because Yesu is the way.

To the mixed accompaniment of hymn singing and the screams and curses of the furious witch doctors, 167 people surrendered their lives to the Lord Jesus. Hallelujah!

On the way home Mebá said, 'Christ always challenges us to do what we feel incapable of doing. He takes delight in the weak.' Then he said something that turned out to be prophetic, 'This church, having come to birth under heavy attack from the Devil, will become strong in the Lord.'

Today the church in Kadjokora is strong and influential and has made an impact on many people in the area. One of the villages they reached with the gospel was Igambo, which was famous for its fetishism.

The unexpected growth of the church, and our own immaturity in ministry, meant that we went through a steep learning curve as we sought to consolidate the church in the two years from February

1996 to the end of 1997. The church recognised the need for discipline after two leaders had to be removed from office in one church due to moral failure. They also saw that a certain level of organisational structure was needed to oversee the growth. Leaders, elders and evangelists met regularly in Koni to study the Word of God, and then began to deal with church problems while they were together.

Meanwhile, I spent two hours a day discipling the evangelists, one day a week training those elders who lived nearby, and two days a month training those from more distant villages.

The social service programme was a natural expression of the outworking of the gospel during those two years. It helped to establish the church as a community of people who were willing to make a difference in society, and has proved to be one of the great chapters in the story of the Church in Koni.

Rossana set up a clinic in Koni that was soon treating around 3,000 patients a year and was a landmark in its demonstration of Christian compassion. A powerful side-effect of the clinic was that it provided a way for the church to begin to take part in the tribal decision-making process in the society. Leaders were frequently invited to participate on the Tribal Council where the most important decisions were made.

Hundreds of children attended the church school where they received a formal education in English. This would help prepare the new generation of Konkombas for their inevitable encounter with modernisation and prevent them from becoming marginalised when rapidly growing villages developed into towns and cities.

Digging wells and widening footpaths so cars could pass also improved the tribe's quality of life, so the church was referred to as a community that shows purpose and compassion to those within the church and to society in general.

We felt these two years of consolidation were vital for establishing the Christian identity within the Konkomba society, so in our teaching we sought to emphasise the essential nature of the church:

- As the community of the redeemed, the Church was brought to birth by God and belongs to God.
- The Church is not an alienating society: those who have been redeemed by Christ and breathe the gospel wherever they are, are still men, women, parents, children, farmers and fishermen.
- The Church is not a community in isolation: we are called to be holy in the world and not apart from it.
- The Church is a community without borders and is therefore missionary.
- The life of the Church, accompanied by the Word, is a great witness to the lost world. It is

necessary that we preach a gospel that makes sense both within and outside the church building.

- ، The major mission of the Church is to glorify the name of God.
- ، The life and thinking of the Church should be centred in the Word of God. The Word never contradicts itself nor the action of God in the Church.

By January 1998, the gospel had touched a vast region. As well as the churches in Koni, Molan and Kadjokora, there were churches in Kimoni, Nabukora, Ipoalim, Mbobo, Sakoni and Bolah and congregations in another three villages. Thirty-five leaders led the churches, including twelve well-trained elders. The Evangelical Church of Ghana set aside four of these to serve the Lord full-time—Labuer, Nprompir, K. Mamah and Iagorá. We continued to spend one day a week training the elders and two hours each day training the full-time evangelists.

The clinic maintained a Christian testimony and the school had 140 pupils. While still consolidating these ministries, Rossana and I began to investigate the possibility of sharing the Word of God in the regions of Naandingoon and Napalbe, but then came news that was like a red rag to a bull! The witch doctors in the villages of Sibru and Bordido sent two messengers to the many villages in the region between the towns of Zabzugu and Tatali, threatening to use fetish power to kill any follower of Christ who tried to pass through their two villages.

The challenge was significant. Sibru and Bordido were fetish centres for a vast area and were unreached with the gospel. Each year, all the local witch doctors made a special trip to Sibru where the head witch doctor gave them new instructions about the sacrifices and major ceremonies. The degree of spiritual power possessed by the Konkomba varies from person to person. Spiritual men, witch doctors, dreamers and healers are the most common. An Ubua (sorcerer) is rarer. Such a person is feared by all and is regarded as totally evil. However, his presence may be needed at the annual meeting of witch doctors whenever serious matters are dealt with.

From Sibru, the witch doctors would walk together to Bordido to make sacrifices to Babasu (Fear) the local fetish which is believed to be the greatest in the region. The site is in an area cleared of weeds, and sacrifices are made on a stone altar at the foot of a narrow outcrop of rock three metres high. On one of the most angular parts of the rock is a dark stain where the blood of the annual sacrifices is poured out. Leaning against the rock are tree trunks on which hang carefully placed bones from both humans and animals.

As one villager pointed out, these tree trunks hold 'not more than one bone from each major sacrifice.'

The growth of the church apparently provoked anxiety among the witch doctors from the villages around Sibru and Bordido. In one of their meetings they decided the power of the fetishes should be re-established through the Bordido fetish. Consequently, they declared Sibru and Bordido would be closed to all Christians. I believe it was the spirits, rather than the witch doctors themselves, who wanted to ban Christians.

It was these threats that prompted us to plan a trip to the villages! On 1 June, several of us went up the Molan River towards Sibru and Bordido, sending a message to Sibru to announce that we were on our way. There was some tension when we failed to get any response. We decided to go ahead, anyway, but found a hostile atmosphere when we arrived in the village. We went into a large, round hut where we found about thirty elders. In front of them stood a very old man who watched us like a hawk. He was Npreem, the village chief.

Initially, I addressed the group in English, which the chief did not understand. Then we noticed the witch doctor, standing next to him and acting as interpreter, was trying to twist my words while translating them. Labuer wisely suggested we speak in Lisachuln, which everybody could understand even though it was not their first language.

Everyone listened with great interest until I started explaining the extent of the messianic promise in

Isaiah 49:5-6. I said, 'Jesus Christ, the promised Messiah, is also Lord of the Konkombas of Sibru and Bordido.' The word for 'Lord' is Tindindann which means 'He who is the owner of the land and reigns over the people.' When I declared that Jesus was Tindindann of the Konkombas of Sibru and Bordido, the witch doctor jumped up angrily. Pointing to a huge round stone, two metres high, which was used for sacrifices, he said, 'We already have Tindindann among us.' Then he stormed out, leaving considerable confusion behind him.

After discussion with the elders, the chief allowed us to speak to the people of both villages. We stayed there for several days. At our first meeting, held under two large trees, we went through the story of creation again, since it is the foundation for any explanation of the gospel. Later we explained the fall and sin, with their respective 'bridges' to understanding. On another occasion we analysed the Old and New Testament teaching about 'Jesus Christ, the beloved Son of God, whose death gives us life.' Iagorá, one of our church leaders, gave a long, detailed personal testimony about how he came to Christ. Consequently twenty-six Konkombas surrendered themselves to Christ the Lord, to the glory of God!

After just three days, the church met for the first time in the village of Bordido. There they sang the hymn, 'The salvation of God is among us.' We decided

Iagorá would stay with the new believers for a while to ground them in the gospel. We also arranged to visit them every two weeks, which was our normal practice with new churches. We then returned to Koni by a different route to avoid a dangerous part of the river, arriving home safely under God's protecting care.

Contrary to the witch doctor's prediction, not a single Christian died in the region of Sibru and Bordido! God answers prayer!

The Holy Spirit at Work

In those first years following the birth of the Konkomba church in the Koni area, we saw various indications of a powerful move of the Holy Spirit. An emphasis on the centrality of the Word of God, an intense passion for Jesus and a high motivation for evangelism are clear evidence of the Holy Spirit at work. At the same time, we saw the church develop a clear understanding of their identity in Christ and of their relationship with each other. We also witnessed the way the church related tribal identity to the Christian's identity in Christ.

The hunger for the Word of God became clear even while people were still painstakingly learning to read. As they gathered in small groups they developed effective ways of hiding the Word in their hearts. One week everyone was memorising Matthew 14:34-6 and they particularly liked the final part, 'and as many as touched it [the hem of Jesus' garment] were made perfectly well.' Some women repeated this short text over and over as they walked to the river to fetch water. Others repeated it while working in the plantations. Even the children were saying it as they played under the trees. The desire to know God's Word was so great that when people living in outlying villages forgot some of the Scriptures they were memorising, they were prepared to walk several kilometres to the nearest believer to ask, 'How does that part go?' Christians set Bible verses to music, singing them repeatedly so they would not forget them.

Many people wanted to learn to read and write. In the evenings they would gather in a circle around a small fire and listen to each other reading portions of the Word to demonstrate what they had learned. No sooner had we begun to teach them to read than they started writing Bible verses all over the place: on jars, walls, trees, anywhere. They did this so they would not 'forget the Lord'. This love for the Scriptures, placing them at the heart of Church life, was a wonderful indication to us of the way the Spirit was moving among the Konkombas.

During the first two years after the birth of the Konkomba church at Koni, new converts were persecuted by their families and by the witch doctors. Many were expelled from their paternal 'compounds' and it was not unusual for believers to lose the rights to their lands. Some believers who were banished from their villages further north sought refuge in Zabzugu where the church was increasing in strength. Some women were threatened by their husbands. In Jimoni, the parents of one young believer locked him in a cage for three weeks. This was done on the instructions of the witch doctor who wanted their son to deny that he had become a follower of Jesus.

Another believer, Bawa, abandoned his fetishes and displayed passionate dedication in following Jesus. Even when he fell seriously ill and his brothers tried to force him to seek healing from the fetishes, he refused to yield. He continued to testify with great joy and fervour until the day of his death.

Some of the leaders received death threats. Meba's enemies made three attempts to poison him.

One young person greatly inspired the first believers in the Koni region. Bifal was a member of the Saboln clan and the son of a witch doctor. He heard about Jesus during one of the open-air meetings, which was held beneath a huge tree in the centre of the village. He was immediately drawn to Jesus and converted.

When he told his family several days later that he was following Jesus, it caused an uproar.

Later his father tried to kill him when he was working in the fields, but he managed to escape and ran home with his father hard on his heels. His mother and brothers protected him, insisting that if he were killed they would all stop worshipping their family fetish! Although Bifal's life was spared, he was banished from the house and forbidden to participate in family life. For several years he wandered from place to place but finally returned to Koni. He continued to follow Jesus and to testify with joy, even though he was still rejected by his family.

Despite the opposition, a contagious joy surged through the veins of every Christian. When we witnessed their unrestrained desire to follow Jesus it edified us tremendously. Jubilation and worship characterised each meeting and a passion for Jesus was obvious in the lives of the saved. They composed dozens of songs expressing what they felt. They had many titles for their Master including Lord of life, Fountain of joy, Way to follow, Motive for living, God that came, Lamb among us, Precious Lord, Hope that never ends, Victorious One, Conqueror of sin and death, and Son like us.

Mebá's enthusiasm and evangelistic fervour fed the church and it seemed almost automatic for the new converts to throw themselves into the task of sharing about their salvation in Jesus Christ. Kidiik used to get so excited when giving his testimony that we tried to avoid having him speak in public because it aroused such strong opposition from the fetishers.

The church was literally on the move because Christians were walking great distances to share the gospel. They were prepared to make sacrifices so that, as one of their songs put it:

> All of the Konkombas might hear,
>   at least once,
> That there is salvation in the person of Jesus.
> He is the Son of God,
> His sacrifice saved us.
> Come Spirit that brings repentance,
> Work in every heart.
> The Church will not stop;
> It's time to speak.

I could give many illustrations of the evangelistic boldness of the Konkomba believers. Tiwaa was about twenty years old. Tall and strong, he was by nature a thinker. He was the first of his clan to come to Jesus and eventually became the worship leader at the Koni church. He suffered all kinds of persecution from his family: he lost his farming rights, he was denied his promised fiancée, his brothers refused to help him in any way and the village witch doctor turned up frequently to curse him. The pressure on Tiwaa was great and we feared for his faith, especially as he was the only believer in the area.

Tiwaa lived on the banks of the Molan River close to Koni. Situated between his house and Koni was the sacred forest, the greatest, and most feared, fetish site in the area. The 'forest' was nothing more than a circle of tall trees surrounding an altar built from three stones. Only the village witch doctor and his helpers were allowed to enter the circle so observers witnessing the sacrifices had to remain outside. Even the soil within the circle was considered sacred. A small amount carried in a little leather sachet hung from the neck or tied to the wrist was thought to give personal protection. However, it became a curse when thrown against the entrance to an enemy's hut.

One day we heard a rumour that Tiwaa had stirred up the anger of the fetish worshippers by going through the sacred forest on his way home one night from a meeting. Surprised, we went to visit him in his compound. Despite an obviously tense atmosphere, we found him sitting there unperturbed by the reaction to what he had done.

He explained why he had gone through the forest: 'Having been saved by Christ, we need to speak about Him to our own people until they understand and get converted. I know, however, that many seek to avoid even hearing about Jesus through fear of the fetishes. During the meeting I thought, "What better way to show that Jesus is greater than the fetishes than by proving that even the sacred forest is inferior to Him?"'

As we did not want to cause unnecessary offence, we counselled Tiwaa not to go through the forest again, but it made no difference. Even though he came under attack from his family and was threatened by the witch doctor and the village chief, he insisted on crossing the forest every time he went to and from the church. After two weeks, his route from the compound to the Koni church was clearly visible. It ran right through the middle of the sacred trees. Nothing happened to Tiwaa and within a few weeks other believers started taking advantage of the new short cut between the village and the river!

Since Tiwaa did not die as predicted, other people, especially members of his clan, were willing to listen to the gospel. The sacred trees lost their power to induce fear and a saying sprung up among the children that reflected this. Translated literally it said,

> The Jesus of Tiwaa,
> Unconcerned,
> Does not fear the sacred forest.
> He is strong.

The evangelistic fervour of the Christians was not limited to sharing the gospel with those who wanted to hear it. Quite often it was necessary to restrain them so that in their enthusiasm they wouldn't force people who were bound by fear to listen to the Word.

It soon became obvious to me that the Konkomba church had been born with an inbuilt calling to be fruitful and multiply. I knew that it would reach out to Konkombas in regions we had never even heard about. By December 1997 thousands of Konkombas had heard about the Lord Jesus, either directly from believers or indirectly by hearsay, and the church had grown. The church was growing in its knowledge of the Word of God, in its devotion to Jesus and in its passion for the lost.

A Christian Identity

The church is also a gathering of people who are part of the body of Christ, and the need to form a 'Christian identity' that would link the individual believer into one body was brought home to me when I heard an account of something that had happened during a recent war.

In September 1993, the Konkombas entered a tribal war against the Dagombas and Gonjas. By the end of 1994, the war had claimed the lives of 10,000 people. We heard many stories, some of which were unsubstantiated, but one story grabbed my attention and prompted me to investigate the emphasis that Konkombas place on their tribal identity.

Nmosingbo was an elderly Konkomba who fled with his family from an attack by the Dagombas. Because he was a cripple he could not keep up with the others and they had to abandon him in the savanna.

Left alone, with only a gourd of water and a handful of dried fish rolled up in a piece of leather, the old man slowly made his way to the shelter of a large tree and sat down on a protruding root. He shuddered when he spotted a group of Dagomba warriors carrying spears and other weapons. Fearing for his life, he probably did what others of his tribe do in the face of death, and began thinking about his ancestors and whispering their names.

During the war many Konkombas had tried to escape attack by not wearing tribal clothes or ornaments. Then, being fluent in the Dagomba language, they could pass as Dagombas when challenged. It did not take the Dagombas long to find a way round this deception. If they suspected that someone was Konkomba, they would rip off his clothes and examine his back for tribal markings. Once his Konkomba identity was confirmed by the presence of two long, horizontal scars, slaughter was inevitable.

When the soldiers spoke to Nmosingbo, he automatically answered in their language. Two young men continued questioning him and became suspicious about his heavy accent on words ending with 'itsh'. They demanded to see his back. As far as Nmosingbo was concerned this was as good as a death sentence. He expected to be killed the moment they saw his tribal markings.

To his amazement, the soldiers simply laughed and went on their way. Not understanding why they had not killed him, Nmosingbo continued his journey eastwards until he arrived at the banks of the Volta River. There he met some women who were also fleeing from the conflict. Together they managed to reach a safe haven. When he told them his story they examined his back. For some reason, possibly because the cuts were made by someone with insufficient experience, the scars had faded over the years until they were now barely detectable.

Rather than rejoicing at his miraculous escape, Nmosingbo promptly sank into deep depression, weeping and crying out, 'I am a Konkomba!' Even though it would have meant certain death, he twice tried to get back to the Dagombas in order to prove his identity by showing them the almost invisible scars. People thought he had gone mad.

Interestingly, Nmosingbo's name means 'What a joy to really be'. Although life was precious to him, being Konkomba was even more precious.

Thinking about this incident prompted us to work on establishing a 'Christian identity' that would link the individual convert in a practical way to the body of the redeemed. It would also mean the church would be a socio-cultural community within the tribe and not alienated from it.

As I heard this story and understood the strength of tribal identity among the Konkombas, I prayed that the Holy Spirit would use this aspect of their culture to strengthen their sense of corporate identity as the body of Christ. The elders discussed this matter at length and identified several areas where ceremonies would contribute to a Konkomba's identification with the church:

Names

Konkomba children are not named until they are about one year old. They are then given a name after a detailed analysis of events at their birth. In a similar way, the church began to have special meetings in which names were given to the offspring of Christian parents. These names were culturally acceptable and reflected what *God* was doing among His people when the child was born.

Even twins, which normally had to follow complex taboos and sacrifices throughout their lives to avoid being killed by evil spirits, began to be accepted by the Christians and given names like any other child.

Marriage

Konkombas have a cyclic rather than a linear worldview and this is reflected in their attitude towards marriage. For them, marriage 'happens' through the years whereas a linear viewpoint requires a visible act with a specific starting date.

Marriages may be arranged with families promising their children to each other soon after birth. Alternatively, 'recognition' involves a form of bride price similar to that which Laban demanded from Jacob. The husband-to-be works for his future father-in-law for many years to pay a 'debt', which could be anything from 500 yams to two farms. As with Jacob, the young man can take his wife while still repaying his debt.

Exchange marriages, where the groom offers his sister to one of his bride's relations as a dowry, did not originate in Konkomba culture; and the church opposes it because it destroys the society.

As we explained God's principles for marriage, the church needed to discover how to apply them to a part of life that was very complex. They began to hold wedding ceremonies, during which they asked for God's blessing on the new family. However, in keeping with the culture, they also saw marriage from a cyclical perspective, so the whole process was divided into culturally acceptable parts: advising young people how to behave, praying over each part of the marriage, and helping the Christian couple to live in God's way within Konkomba culture.

Feast of new yams

Konkombas celebrate the harvesting of new yams with a special feast. During this time there is a tremendous emphasis on the occult, and collective possession by spirits may occur under the leadership of a group of witch doctors from the region. The church suggested believers celebrate the harvest by bringing their first fruits to a special service in which they could thank the Lord for the harvest and pray for the next planting.

Offerings

Before the gospel arrived, it was common practice for villagers to give offerings to their witch doctors, traditional healers and diviners, so it was not difficult for believers to accept the idea of giving a tenth of their produce to the Lord. They brought their tithes of yams, manioc, corn, chickens, pigs, and money, according to the harvest or the birth of animals.

Funerals

All Konkombas dream of having many children and living to a ripe old age. They also dream of having many people dancing at their funeral. The church adopted a procedure for funerals that maintained this cultural aspect but, in place of the songs designed to invoke the spirits, they sang choruses. Sometimes the Christians composed Konkomba-style hymns that glorified the name of the Lord and spoke about the reality of the believer's life with God after death.

A Konkomba funeral is performed in several stages that can take years to complete. When a man dies, his widow is locked in a hut with his body and forbidden to eat anything for the rest of the day. For three days she is not permitted to bathe. During that time everyone in the compound has to be careful to keep silent at dusk so that the spirits will not speak to them.

The first funeral is called Lisaton and takes place three days after the death of a man. The second funeral, the Unhobuabor, held six months later, can last for five days and is a time when everyone comes to dance, sing and drink.

The third funeral or Ubualiliir takes place two years after the death. This is the time when the widow is obliged to marry her oldest brother-in-law after going through a private ritual for three days.

The final funeral, the Ubuadja, is celebrated around ten to fifteen years after the death. After this ceremony, the widow is entitled to be called an Upupijor or 'Keeper of the rules of conduct of women'.

Kidiik's mother, Awar, was thrown into this complex world of funeral customs when she was widowed. Although a funeral is meant to reflect the meaning of life for a Konkomba, Awar became restless and frustrated. She remembered what Kidiik and Labuer had told her about Jesus and this led her to start thinking beyond her cultural horizons. The attraction of the gospel grew and her understanding of the significance of the death, burial, and resurrection of Christ increased. Awar was so passionate in her surrender to Jesus that someone wrote a song about her expression of joy:

> I'm walking with Jesus.
> Happiness.
> I'm walking with Jesus.

BIBLE TRANSLATION

Although the church in our area was very much alive, there was a nagging sensation that something vital was missing. Because the Word of God was not yet available in the dialect of the Bimonkpeln Konkombas, the young church was dependent on our continued presence. Although some of the church leaders who were familiar with the Lichabol dialect were using the Lichabol Bible that had been translated by a Wycliffe team, the Christians longed for a translation in their own native tongue. We became aware of this need when talking with a Limonkpeln Konkomba about the Bible. He said wistfully, 'I can hardly imagine the sensation of reading all this in my own language!'

Bible translation has unquestionable value. It makes the Word of God accessible to many people rather than just a few. While it is true that people who know more than one language can read the Bible in their second language, it becomes much sweeter and speaks more convincingly about sin and grace when they read it in their heart language.

From the cultural point of view, a translation enhances the conviction that people are of value to God just as they are. So Konkombas do not need to become white people or southerners in order for God to speak their language.

Pastor Ghuntger, who translated the Bible for the Xerente people of Brazil in the mid-twentieth century, beautifully described the experience of someone reading the Word of God in his own language for the first time as like 'being alone and lost in a foreign country when suddenly you hear someone call out your name in your own language.'

Finally, there is the testimony of years, even decades or generations, of hard work. Translation work is never an easy job, and neither is Bible translation. However, those who receive the Word are blessed by the story of how it came to them; a story that is neither brief nor simple.

As the church grew, we did some rough translations of Scripture portions into Limonkpeln, but it was not long before it became apparent that these brief translations were insufficient for the spiritual demand. The people had innumerable questions and we were obliged to translate Matthew, Acts and Romans in order to give the facts about the life of Jesus and the early Church as well as the basic doctrines of Christianity. The people received these books with great excitement and memorized large blocks of Scripture. They learned to love the Word and had lengthy meetings in which they discussed how to apply it.

When we began the translation work, Labuer and I used to sit under a tree near my house for three or four hours a day, working on various texts. Over the years others decided to join us to make the dream of having a Limonkpeln Bible come true. Besides Labuer, I must mention the incredible and zealous work of Peter Balabon, Timothy Kunjon Yajool, Timothy Naasan, James Damba and the much loved 'big' James. These dear ones formed the translation team. They were dedicated to the task and on several occasions worked day and night without a break. For more than seven years, probably not a single day passed without someone working on the New Testament text.

The church, seeing us struggling with the translation, began to pray that they might soon have the whole New Testament in their language. This put me under some pressure. Who wouldn't feel pressurised when the church was praying and fasting to see the job finished! Every day we were faced with the same agonising question: 'When do you think you will eventually finish the work so that we can have the Word of God?' If I decided to take an afternoon off to play with the children, I began to feel ashamed and even a little slack. When some members of the church silently watched us, I felt as though they were censuring me. Finally, I felt compelled to give priority to the translation work. Whenever possible, I worked at night because it was much cooler then and I could enjoy the much-needed quietness after everyone else had gone to sleep.

Having completed the translation of Romans in record time, we faced the nerve-racking audit by Bible Society consultants. While it is standard practice for new translations to be checked for accuracy and readability, I could not help feeling like a first-year schoolboy being questioned by the headmistress! So it was a real relief, after two weeks of seeing our work carefully examined, to hear the consultants give their wholehearted approval to it.

Alongside the emphasis on Bible translation, we placed an equally strong emphasis on the related task of teaching people to read in their native language. When we set up a Limonkpeln reading programme for adults in the Koni area many Bimonkpeln Konkombas made the most of the opportunity to learn to read and write.

By January 1998, three hundred people had learnt to read and write well in their own language after taking part in the adult literacy programme. We had also translated Luke and were now working on Hebrews.

The Word of God helped the church to mature. The contact with the Scriptures helped the church to take its stand in society and develop its own theology. In the light of their analysis of the text, the Elders' Council began applying Biblical theology to controversial and difficult matters such as the stance of the church towards polygamy, tribal warfare and the fetish obligation to circumcise infants. They also tackled the problem of exchange marriages, which results in two marriages that are so interlinked that if one breaks down, the other automatically terminates as well.

It was common to see the converted Konkombas going to the rivers or fields reciting the verses they had memorized the previous day. Some of them turned the verses into songs so they wouldn't forget them, others used them in the stories they told round the open fire in the evenings, while yet others remembered Konkomba proverbs or stories that illustrated certain biblical truths.

After hearing us speak about the enemy's strategies to confuse God's people from 1 Peter 5:8, 'Be self-controlled and alert. Your enemy, the devil, prowls around like a roaring lion looking for someone to devour', two Konkombas and a Bassari told us an Ashanti story that illustrated the activity of the enemy.

There were once three friends: the lion, the leopard and the python. None of them was perfect: the lion had a phobia about getting dirty, the leopard hated being stared at, and the python had a fear of being trodden on.

One day, they came together for a meeting, and then took a nap after their meal. A tiny doodlebug had overheard them promising never to offend each other, and mischievously decided to test their loyalty. He crept up to the lion and began to dig a pit, throwing dirt onto his nose. The lion jumped up, stared at the leopard and accused his friend of making him dirty. The two animals started fighting and in the process, the leopard stepped on the python, who joined in the fight. All three animals died in the ensuing battle. The whole forest was stunned. How could such kind, gentle and responsible leaders reach the point of killing each another?

'The devil is like the doodlebug,' said the Konkombas. 'He only comes to kill, steal and destroy!'

God Is Building His Church

The Konkomba Church in the Koni area was by no means always joyful and victorious in its early years. There were moments of sadness, defeat, problems among the leaders, and occasions when people needed to be disciplined. But even in the hard times, the Holy Spirit continued to manifest Himself in a tremendous way among us. The church grew numerically and we experienced God's anointing.

As a family we, too, passed through times of frustration and anxiety and I could speak for days about the problems we faced: persecution, poisoning, sickness, misfortune and oppression. In particular, I suffered from repeated attacks of malaria. Doubtless, many of our problems were evidence of spiritual opposition to our work, but God was using my frequent illnesses to achieve His purposes!

Although we were working among the Bimonkpeln in Ghana, we wanted to start a church-planting movement among the Konkomba who lived over the border in the neighbouring country of Togo. However, every time we tried to get something organised, I got another attack of malaria, obliging us to stay in Ghana. Because it always took me a long time to recover, I used the time to work on the Bible translation. It was much later that Rossana and I realised that the four years in which I had suffered so much sickness had proved to be productive in translating the New Testament! We saw then that it was this work that was God's priority. As for the Konkomba in Togo, the Koni church has since sent several evangelists across the border—armed with God's Word!

Eventually, sickness obliged us to leave the country. After four years of working with the Konkomba, I contracted spinal tuberculosis. The diagnosis was confirmed in April 1998, and I realised I would need to return to Brazil for treatment. The prospect of a premature departure was unsettling: we could see so much that still needed to be done and we were anxious about the church. I struggled on until June. By that time the pain in my back was so severe I had great difficulty in walking and driving. The believers would have to go on without us.

Back in Brazil, I continued to work on the translation. For another three and a half years I plodded on, spending hours on end in front of the computer, surrounded by books and deep in thought. Rossana and the children were supportive and uncomplaining about the time I spent in translation. Ronaldo Junior, who was just two-years-old when we left Ghana, grew so used to this work that whenever he was asked where I was, quickly responded, 'My dad is at the computer making a Bible,' whether I was doing that or not!

Eventually the work was completed. One day I gathered all the material we used in the translation, from the first drafts through to the final copies. Each book had been corrected from beginning to end—five times! There were over thirty reference books, piles of paper, and countless letters written in Portuguese, English and Limonkpeln, not to mention hundreds of emails exchanged with language consultants. It was hard to believe the result of all this could fit into the palm of my hand on one simple CD!

When I handed over the finished text I thought my feelings would lie somewhere between joy and relief, but the overriding emotion turned out to be anxiety. How accurate was our work? Could I have improved the expression used for 'long-suffering?' Had it been wise to use the same term as the traditional spirit-worshippers used when speaking of sacrifice? The Word of God is the sword of the Spirit and is a vital part of the armour that God gives to His children. It is not surprising then that the translation, publication and distribution of the Scriptures is often opposed by the evil one. Christians who had far more experience than we did in spiritual warfare repeatedly warned us that there would be a time of intense enemy attack when the New Testament was published and distributed. Heeding their advice, we asked people to pray. So when we returned to Ghana in 2004 for the dedication of the Limonkpeln New Testament, the church in Brazil was praying, our fellow WECers in Ghana and other parts of the world were praying, the Konkomba church was praying—and God heard their prayers. The eagerly-awaited dedication, to be held in the district capital of Kpassah, was scheduled for 24 October and the entire WEC team in Ghana was mobilized to help with the preparations. Everyone was looking forward to this special celebration, and the enemy knew it well.

Before going to Kpassah for the dedication, Rossana and I wanted to spend a few days visiting our friends in Koni. The Dueck family kindly lent us their air-conditioned car and we set off. In the car with us were our dear friends Nkrumah and Grace, with their two little girls, one still a baby.

A few kilometres away from Koni our car got bogged down in mud. While Rossana stayed in the car with Grace and the children, Nkrumah and I went to look for wood to put under the wheels. Suddenly, we were attacked by a great swarm of bees. Believing the others would be safe as long as they stayed in the car with the windows up, Nkrumah and I ran for our lives.

But when I turned round, at a safe distance, I was horrified to see the huge swarm of bees hovering round the car. It showed no sign of moving away and I was overcome with concern for Rossana, afraid that bees had managed to get inside the car. I ran back towards the car. As I did so, the bees attacked me so viciously that I fell three times before reaching it; but God helped me, giving me enough strength to reach the car and struggle inside.

With the car still bogged down there was nothing we could do but sit there and bide our time until the bees decided to leave. The engine overheated so Rossana had to switch it off with the result that we no longer had air-conditioning. Despite the incredible heat, everyone else seemed to be all right. (A few bees had got into the car, but had been quickly swatted.) A few minutes later, I started to feel terrible. The poison from about a hundred bee stings made my heart race and I could hardly breathe. I started blacking out and having convulsions so Rossana poured cold water over my head in a desperate attempt to keep me awake. Grace spent the time calling on the name of Jesus. As the hours passed, death seemed inevitable. During a lucid moment I said goodbye to Rossana and gave her a final message for our children telling them how much I loved them.

News of the attack reached the elderly witch doctor in a nearby village. He claimed to have called up the bees to attack someone else, but decided to profit from our plight. He sent a messenger, swathed in cloths, to the car. Pressing his face against the window, he yelled, 'The witch doctor says to tell the white man that he called up these bees. If he promises to pay him with some strong drink he will make them go away.' I was so ill that I didn't understand his message at first. Then God intervened mightily to deliver us from what was obviously a snare set by the enemy. For two minutes I felt incredibly well: I could breathe again, and the nausea disappeared. This enabled me to think clearly enough to realise that the enemy was attempting to discredit the power of the Word just as it was arriving in written form.

If the bearers of the translated Word of God had died because of being attacked by bees, it would undoubtedly have been interpreted as a testimony of faithfulness. On the other hand, imagine the reaction if we had accepted the deceptive offer of the witch-doctor in that moment of desperation! It would have been a profound defeat for the gospel. As God gave me His strength, I managed to respond by saying that as far as we were concerned we would pray only to Him.

Following this, the convulsions returned with greater intensity while the bees continued circling the car. In my confusion, I opened the door and jumped out, telling Rossana that I would rather die outside. She also got out and at that moment Nkrumah suddenly reappeared. He half carried me for two kilometres as we ran towards a stream. There I collapsed, drifting in and out of consciousness, while the others bathed my head and washed away some of the stings. Just as I seemed about to take my last breath, Makanda, Mark and Émmanuel arrived with some antihistamine, which eased my breathing. When I regained consciousness I was in our house at Koni. Later, when I had a shower, dozens of stings were flushed out of my hair and body.

When the Koni witch doctor heard what had happened, he went to see the old witch doctor to ask if he had deliberately summoned the bees to attack me. The old man said he had not because he knew that I was a good man who had helped the community by building the clinic. He said he had summoned the bees to attack three of his enemies. The plan backfired. First the bees went into the old man's village and caused havoc there, and later they returned and attacked the old man himself. The Koni witch doctor then came to see me and apologised for what had happened.

The attack happened on a Friday and just two days later, much to everyone's amazement, I was strong enough to preach at the Sunday morning service. That afternoon I went to visit the old man who had called up the bees. When I saw how swollen his face and body were, I realised how gracious God had been to me because my face did not swell at all.

Following the attack, I suffered from flashbacks and pains in my left arm and if I stood for too long I became dizzy. But I praise the Lord that I recovered enough to attend the dedication of the New Testament ten days later.

The day started at 10am and the people celebrated with singing and dancing in true Konkomba style for almost six hours until dark clouds warned us that a big storm was on its way. When the first batch of 200 New Testaments was unveiled there was great excitement and the Christians danced for joy round the piles of precious books. The excitement mounted as the first five copies were sold by auction! Then there was a great rush to buy the remaining copies. By evening every New Testament had been sold.

The joy of the Bimonkpeln Christians as they received the Word of God in their own language was immense. Rossana said, 'They received the New Testaments as if they were bars of gold.'

Hundreds of people praised God with unspeakable joy because, as one teenage lad explained, 'God speaks Limonkpeln!'

More New Testaments would arrive later and one member of the translation team was made responsible for their shipment to all forty-eight regions, including sixteen in Togo, where Limonkpeln is spoken.

After the celebration we returned to the Duecks' house. The next day a messenger came from a village known for its resistance to the gospel. Speaking for the village chief, the man said, 'We know that God's Book speaks Limonkpeln. That's our language. We want to hear it!'

Once again our hearts were filled with joy as we grasped the precious significance of this request. God's Word can pass through all kinds of barriers. When it is translated into the heart language of a people, it enters resistant villages, captivates the hearts of those who are far away and leaves a legacy that will long outlive the translator.

As I looked back on our years among the Konkomba, I remembered something that God had done in one particular resistant region.

Around Ketiman the people had resisted the gospel for two years, not even allowing us to enter their villages. However, shortly before our departure in 1998, we heard the head witch doctor there had died. Knowing that it would be at least six months before a new one would be recognised, we believed that this was the right moment to attempt another visit. After a tricky 're-entry' we were able to explain the gospel to a few small groups.

Following a period of pre-evangelism, we held an open-air meeting in which six people surrendered themselves to Jesus despite strong opposition from the fetish worshippers. This little group of new believers was headed by Amina, a widow who quickly became the prime focus for persecution. We returned to Koni, leaving Kimana, our youngest evangelist, to spend a few days giving more teaching to the new Christians.

One week later, one of the new converts arrived in our village and asked us to return to Ketiman with him immediately. Thinking there must be a problem, we were amazed when he explained that after Kimana left, Amina had gone from hut to hut evangelising the rest of the village and a further sixty people had come to the Lord Jesus!

Perhaps this incident was on Labuer's mind on the day that we prepared to leave all the celebrations and return to our new church-planting ministry among the Amazon Indians in Brazil. Along with the other elders, Labuer came to our house to pray for us. He closed his farewell prayer by saying, 'It is Jesus who is building His church.' This brief word ministered peace into our hearts as we left the village behind us.

Whether it is through the hard slog of translation, or the simple witness of an excited new believer, it is indeed the Lord Jesus Christ who is building His church on earth, to the glory of God the Father. Hallelujah!

African Fable

This is the full story quoted in chapter nine. I have done my best to translate both accurately and literally, adapting Konkomba expressions that do not have an English equivalent.

In the jungle beside the Molan River there lived a wise old lion who, as leader of the animals that inhabited the earth, was greatly respected by everyone. Due to his many years of leadership experience he had developed a personality that was patient, meticulous and steady to the point of being almost contemplative. Nevertheless he was taken very seriously by everyone when he raised himself up from his favourite clump of bushes to speak in his usual fashion: 'I believe that I know what ought to be done.'

Even his rivals, who criticised his pacifying manner, saw in him a fountain of wisdom. There was only one almost imperceptible defect in his personality, and since it was so tiny no one considered it a defect, but rather an eccentricity—'even a virtue', many said—the lion hated dirt! Mud, food scraps or even ordinary dust made him irritated and unhappy. Nevertheless, it wasn't sufficient to cause disagreements or debates; at the most he gave a sign of disapproval by the shaking of his head or by a quick sigh of indignation.

Downriver, high up in a tree with few leaves, lived a large leopard. He was lithe and very alert. Being a cheerful fellow, he liked to tell jokes, particularly funny stories about the river dwellers. As he was the only animal of any size in that part of the forest, he was always called upon in an emergency; although he lacked the thoughtfulness and experience of the lion, he generally came up with some solutions, making a joke of the problems, which then seemed less serious. He hardly ever used his authority as the strongest one of all, and liked to walk around each afternoon promising the monkeys that they would be his next day's meal if nothing better turned up. This always caused a stir in the trees while he laughed and laughed.

Although he was a friend and companion of the other animals, there was something that hindered his having a closer relationship with them: he became really angry every time someone stared at him. He could talk for hours with everyone as long as nobody looked him straight in the eye, because then he would get angry and, with a roar, would walk off in a huff. But since everyone was aware of this peculiarity, they knew how to deal with him. They even joked among themselves, saying that he had been like that since he came face to face with his own image reflected in the water of the Molan River and noticed with surprise how ugly he was. This was just one of the versions the monkeys used to tell to amuse themselves in the evenings. However, being aware of his temperament beforehand, everyone knew how to deal with it, so everything went along smoothly in that part of the jungle.

Further away, near the swamp of the 'High Tree' lived the python. He was the biggest, strongest and most intelligent of all the many snakes that dwelt in the area. Although feared by all the animals, the python wasn't as hard to get along with as many imagined. He was serious, a deep thinker, but without a doubt, very distrusting. However, he had always shown himself ready to help in moments of crisis.

'When we had our last flood,' everyone admitted, 'the python was the first to volunteer to help the animals that couldn't swim.'

'But he keeps talking about it, even now!' added his more severe critics. Even though he had neither the wisdom of the lion nor the good humour of the leopard, the python was recognised as a leader.

'A leader should never be feared, hard to get on with or distrustful,' the monkeys reminded everyone, indicating that if they could, they would remove him from leadership. It was well known that the python had a huge phobia about being stepped on because he was much lower than the other animals and had to slither along the ground. Once, an elephant almost stepped on him because it didn't see him, and this caused him great indignation. From that time on, he couldn't bear being touched and always reminded everyone: 'Never step on me.'

One day an urgent matter came up involving the whole forest. Some hyenas, feared by all the animals of goodwill, decided to move into the region. Everyone was worried and this led to many rumours and much gossip about the matter. The lion, foreseeing a panic, decided to call a gathering of the leadership of the forest the following day. They would meet in his clump of trees.

Early the following day, the leopard arrived and, as was his custom, made jokes about the lion, calling him 'Mini-Mane', a somewhat hot issue rarely mentioned by the other animals. The lion had been born with much less hair on his mane than others of his species. Pretending to ignore the jokes, the lion called the leopard over to his clump of trees and offered him water from the creek that flowed there.

Soon afterwards, the python slithered in subtly and with his head high. The lion was surprised. 'I didn't think you would come so early,' he commented, referring to the way the python had arrived late at recent meetings of the leadership. As usual the python didn't say a word, and calmly looked for the most humid place to curl up in.

Throughout the day, the lion, the leopard and the python talked about all the implications of the hyenas moving into their forest. After listening patiently to endless suggestions from the other animals, they were ready to make a decision when they were interrupted by the arrival of food.

'I thought the lion's plan was to bring us here to starve us to death,' commented the leopard, smiling. They ate splendidly and after cleaning up everything they decided to have a rest for a while before resuming discussions.

As the lion, the leopard and the python were sleeping, a tiny doodlebug who had overheard them promising never to offend each other, mischievously decided to test their loyalty. He crept up to where the lion was lying on his lovely, clean, soft clump of grass and began to dig a pit, throwing dirt onto the lion's nose. When the lion smelled the dust, he leapt up, thinking the leopard was playing a joke on him. Glaring at him, he roared: 'Why did you throw dust on me? You know I detest dirt!'

The leopard snarled indignantly: 'I don't know what you're talking about, but you know that I hate anyone staring at me!'

The two of them began to fight but, not seeing the python, the leopard stepped on him with his back foot, which made him wake up angry and yelling, 'I won't tolerate anyone treading on me!'

The leopard, younger and stronger, killed the lion in a tremendous battle. The python, in his wisdom, wrapped himself round the leopard and squeezed him till he died. However, the effort was too much for him and he also died.

There was silence throughout the whole forest. 'How could such kind, responsible leaders come to the point of killing one another?' everyone asked. The forest animals, frightened and with their heads down, scattered. And the doodlebug . . .

After everything was over, the doodlebug came out of his little hole in the sand, looked around and began to hop off towards the next valley, in search of other leaders in other forests.

'The devil is like the doodlebug. He only comes to kill, steal and destroy!' say the Konkombas.

Tribal Wars

A tribal war scars a society for years. By the time we left Ghana in 1998, Konkombas, Dagombas, Gonjas and other tribes had been involved in frequent periods of warfare for more than a decade. No one has been able to determine the precise causes of the most recent conflicts, but they all stemmed from some minor event such as the theft of a chicken, someone trespassing in a field, or even a misunderstanding during a conversation.

When threatened or cornered, the Konkombas suddenly become dangerous human fighting machines. They have several advantages when it comes to fighting. Unlike the Dagombas and Gonjas, who have specific clans of warriors set apart for attack and defence, every Konkomba man, from the youngest to the oldest, enlists when the tribe is under threat. Men who are too old to fight contribute by taking supplies from the villages to the front lines.

Not only are they able to move at great speed across the savannah, but they can also mobilise themselves impressively quickly. When a Konkomba wants to raise an alarm, he uses a guttural cry that sets off a chain reaction. As soon as a fellow Konkomba hears it, he runs to help while repeating the cry. This quickly brings help from all directions in ever-increasing circles. In no time at all, an impressive group of warriors, many armed for conflict, surround the spot where the first alarm was sounded. This strategy became well known in the whole north-eastern region where one simple alarm led to many enemy troops being surrounded almost as soon as they were discovered. I am convinced that one reason for the Konkombas' power is their unity and that everyone is involved in the warfare.

Konkombas keep their weapons (bows and arrows or rifles) well guarded. Most families use one hut on their compound in which to hide weapons. Often this is the place where fetishes and amulets are kept, because conflicts are associated with spiritual forces. Weapons are hung up in the thatch, hidden from view unless you look really closely.

Amulets, hung round the neck or tied to the wrist of the hand that holds the bow, are considered an essential part of warfare. These small leather sachets filled with sacred earth are charms linked to protecting spirits. At birth each Konkomba receives a name linking them to one of these spirits. As the child grows, the witch doctor will indicate which amulet must be used for protection. Some amulets are meant to protect the body and in such cases it is said the person is 'shut up' against any attack. Some people believe that their amulets will even make them disappear when danger is imminent. Many Konkombas have been killed in foolhardy attacks because they trusted their charms for protection.

In preparation for coming conflict, a Konkomba warrior oils his whole body to make it difficult for his enemy to get a grip in hand-to-hand combat. He also takes a drug that has the dual effect of numbing the brain and stimulating aggression for several hours. Under its influence the warrior is capable of terrifying savagery. Victims have been brutally tortured, burned alive, or beheaded and their heads impaled on spears.

The fetishes take centre stage in every conflict. In our region, Kayaan, the fetish linked to death and war, receives sacrifices in which many animals are killed according to the instructions of the witch doctor. Normally, however, each person also seeks protection from the fetish of his own clan.

Because tribal warfare has such strong links to the fetish, any conflict has significant implications for the local church. When the Konkombas were fighting the Dagombas and Nanumbas, the Christians expressed their desire not to join the conflict. The traditional elders of some of the villages to the north of the Oti River gathered to discuss the church's attitude. They then gave the Christians an ultimatum: if they did not participate in the combat, they would not be protected from attack. The church stood firm in its decision, believing that these conflicts are in reality strategies of the Devil to destroy the lives of people who have not yet heard the message of Jesus.

Missionary Communication and Church Growth

A missiological perspective

Before looking at cross-cultural issues linked to the rapid growth of the Konkomba Church, I would like to make some important observations about missionary communication:

1. It is not the reason for the growth of the church, but rather a tool for faithfully transmitting the

message that has been entrusted to us. The generating power behind church growth is the action of the Holy Spirit.

2 The success of a mission cannot be defined exclusively by the results obtained (i.e. growth of the church) but should also be defined by the faithfulness demonstrated in communicating the gospel.

3 Character is more important than human ability. The life of the missionary undoubtedly speaks much more loudly than formal linguistic communication. Actions really do speak louder than words!

In the work of planting the Konkomba Church, we became increasingly aware of certain cross-cultural issues that acted as bridges of influence into local society. We sought to implement them in our approach.

a We used Limonkpeln, the language of the people, to communicate the message rather than Lichabol, the more widely spoken, general Konkomba language.

b We encouraged the use of the local language when composing songs, and avoided songs in Twi (a highly influential language from the south of Ghana) as much as possible. Although music and dance linked to the culture and society were used in worship, we took great care to avoid any suggestion of syncretism.

c We made it clear from the first explanation of the Word of God that the gospel provokes changes in the culture. Again we emphasized this in order to avoid forming a church bordering on syncretism. We taught that changes are not necessarily opposed to culture if society chooses them, because every society has the liberty to review its customs and make cultural changes.

d Once scripture had been translated, we used culturally related materials when applying biblical truth. These included stories, myths, proverbs and music to ensure that people would understand the message in their culture and put it into practice from day to day.

e We stressed local leadership from the beginning to facilitate a better bridge of communication. Even recently appointed elders often explained biblical concepts and their cultural implications far better than we could.

f Biblical exposition preceded practical theology and the development of church practice. The missionary's job was centred on biblical exposition. Local Christians, especially elders, were then able to suggest excellent practical applications of biblical concepts ninety per cent of the time. Only rarely did the missionary have to intervene and put them right.

g We placed a major emphasis on social work. In the Konkomba universe—as in the world of all mankind—it would be impossible to understand how a Christian could love the soul while ignoring the suffering of the body. Health projects, boring wells, formal education for children and adult literacy programmes brought life to the people and gave them the opportunity to 'confirm our words through our actions'. Thousands of patients were treated at the clinic and this contributed to the evangelistic process. Some women came to know Jesus during their treatment and the impact of their conversions brought others to Jesus. Many people, especially those suffering from epilepsy (a sickness considered by the tribe to be a spiritual attack), were touched by the Lord and surrendered themselves to Him.

Anthropological perspective

A culture may contain elements that appear bizarre to outsiders. If missionary communication is to be effective, we need to understand such phenomena. If we fail to exercise spiritual discernment, we put ourselves in danger of either permitting syncretism or condemning innocent practices. When examining unusual elements of a culture, we need to keep in mind three essential principles.

Not everything that is different is religious

Missionaries have a tendency to give religious interpretations to any unusual activity in a culture. I call this a 'spirit-phenomenological neurosis'! It reflects a failure to realise that a society has to deal with the practicalities of everyday life as well as practising its religion.

To give an example, the Bassari tribe (neighbours of the Konkombas) perform a complicated ritual when someone dies. Using a wooden scoop, they constantly pour a mixture of water and fat over the body. Green leaves are thrown into the flames of a fire as people gather round and seemingly 'recite' certain words. Twenty years ago, one missionary concluded that this was 'an act of invoking demons in order to ask the spirits to guide the one who died', but the truth is different!

Although most of the Bassari follow traditional religion and are under powerful influences of evil, the basis for this particular ritual is very mundane. The mixture of water and fat slows the decomposition of the body, preserving it until relatives arrive from distant villages. Burning green leaves produces smoke that drives away mosquitoes and, as for gathering round the fire, this is a normal evening ritual in a society without electric lights. The words spoken are probably simply greetings to new arrivals.

The so-called religious act is merely a cultural-scientific process.

Not everything ceremonial is demonic

There are two opposing points of view that are destructive to missionary work: disbelief in demonic activity and belief that everything is demonic. To understand whether or not something is demonic we can use theology, missiological knowledge, observation and wisdom. However, problems arise for the missionary when the gospel has only recently touched a society. To communicate the gospel in an effective way, it is necessary to grasp quickly the significance of the culture's religious phenomena. This is not easy when the workers have had little exposure to the local culture. The only solution is a daily dependence on God for spiritual discernment.

Not everything that is cultural is pure

Anthropologists frequently claim that untouched cultures have a 'natural purity'. This belief can have an impact on cross-cultural communication.

It is important to remember that sin invades culture along with every other aspect of human life. It springs out of the human heart, wraps itself in concepts and customs, and manifests itself through language, culture and the environment. Ever since the fall of man, sin has led to an abyss separating mankind from a Holy God. In every sin-contaminated culture, mankind needs redemption.

We did not stumble upon a paradise of cultural purity among the Konkombas. Instead we found a people who appeared happy but in reality were bowed down before the enemy and experiencing something of hell on earth. Desperate for some kind of redemption, if only temporary, they sought for it through sacrifices, idols, charms, taboos, magic and demonic rituals.

We know that true redemption is found only in Jesus. This is the gospel message. And passing it on to others is called mission!

A Brief History of WEC in Ghana

WEC missionaries entered the British Protectorate of the Northern Territories in 1940, and the District Commissioner helped them to obtain a plot of land at Tuna. From here they went out on treks to evangelise the villages. People were keen to listen, but there was little genuine response. Their first real breakthrough came at the end of 1941, when the chief of Tuna said that he wanted to finish with witchcraft and follow God's way. In 1942 Don Theobald and Leslie Seaman undertook a great trek to explore the whole Gonja district in which Tuna was located, an area of about 370 by 260 kilometres in the north-east of Ghana bordering Togo. They found that the homeland of the Gonja people was also home to many other peoples, including the Konkomba. The vision was born to evangelise the whole district, and an appeal went out for new workers.

The team opened a new base at Kpandai in the east, about 480 kilometres by road from Tuna. They saw their first convert in Kpandai in 1946. By 1947 the number of workers had increased to seven. At the request of the British Government, they launched a programme to treat leprosy patients, setting up treatment centres, outreach clinics, a big leprosarium and a farm. Because the goal was evangelism, the leprosy patients always heard the gospel when they came for treatment. At first the results were disappointing, but the persevering love of the missionaries opened the hearts of people, some of whom later became leaders of the first churches. They saw a harvest among the Konkomba people in the Kpandai area and Damongo.

In 1959 Don Theobald opened a Bible school at Kpandai to train national workers. Later, other schools were opened at Tuna and Damongo. At this stage the church was known as The Peoples' Church.

Four years later, a radio ministry was started at Kpandai. By 1967 it had expanded to include a liter-ature ministry and a Bible correspondence course. This ministry moved south to Kumasi, where a large plot of land was obtained in 1969, in order to have access to better facilities and national contributors. This brought WEC into contact with Christians in the south who were concerned about their country's unevangelised peoples.

Ultimately, this led to the opening of the Christian Service College in 1974. The College was governed by a Ghanaian council. National Christians formed the Christian Outreach Fellowship to recruit Ghanaian missionaries. A Ghana Evangelism Committee was also formed, which launched 'New Life for All' as a joint-church project in 1975. Thousands of Christians attended retreats where God renewed their zeal for evangelism, and many nominal churchgoers were converted.

Meanwhile the work continued in northern Ghana. A new station opened at Buipe in the central Gonja area, and in 1969 Jeanette Zwart arrived to learn the Gonja language and translate the New Testament.

In 1977 the seventeen national church leaders held their first council. They wrote a constitution and elected a president so that the church could be legally registered as the Evangelical Church of Ghana (ECG).

In the 1980s, missionaries concentrated on learning the languages and cultures of specific peoples, including the Frafra people of the north-east, and later the Dagomba who had shown little response to the gospel. A survey, conducted by the Ghana Evangelism Committee, highlighted a migration of northern peoples to towns in the south. When WEC began church planting in these communities, the Frafra people were very responsive to their message.

From 1985 the ECG grew rapidly. To deal with the acute need for leadership training, a programme of Theological Training by Extension was introduced. Growth has slowed over recent years, but currently there are about 6,000 members, 130 congregations and 60 pastors.

WEC Ghana continues to work in close partnership with the ECG to bring the church to maturity and independence. In addition to training pastors and elders, WEC missionaries have been involved in establishing the women's, children's and youth ministries of the ECG. A vocational school and computer training centre have been set up in Accra, and schools have been built in some of the northern towns to give ECG members better opportunities for education and employment. Medical work continues through the Kpandai health centre and Koni health post.

In co-operation with the Ghanaian Institution of Linguistics, Literacy and Bible Translation, WEC workers are also engaged in Bible translation, particularly among the Birifor people.

Because the task of evangelising the peoples of Ghana is far from complete, so me missionaries are still involved in pioneering church planting.

About WEC

WEC International has over 1800 workers drawn from over 40 countries in over 70 countries of the world. From its beginnings in the Congo in 1913 it has grown to work in many parts of the world. Evangelical and inter-denominational in outlook, WEC's ethos is based on Four Pillars of Faith, Sacrifice, Holiness, and Fellowship. WEC's commission is to bring the gospel of our Lord Jesus Christ to the remaining unevangelised peoples of the world with utmost urgency, to demonstrate the compassion of Christ to a needy world, to plant churches and lead them to spiritual maturity, and to inspire, mobilise and train for cross-cultural mission.

To help us achieve that, we have 16 Sending Bases scattered throughout the world which recruit, screen, send and help support workers. We also train missionary workers at six training institutes around the world.

WEC workers are involved in almost every type of direct outreach and support ministry related to the fulfilment of these aims. WEC's ministries range from the International Research Office that produces the prayer handbook *Operation World*, through the planting and establishment of churches, to the enabling of national missionary sending agencies in mature WEC fields.

Our Lifestyle

- We fervently desire to see Christ formed in us so that we live holy lives.
- In dependence on the Holy Spirit we determine to obey our Lord whatever the cost.
- We trust God completely to meet every need and challenge we face in His service.
- We are committed to oneness, fellowship and the care of our whole missionary family.

Our Convictions

- We are convinced that prayer is a priority.
- We uphold biblical truth and standards.
- We affirm our love for Christ's Church, and endeavour to work in fellowship with local and national churches, and with other Christian agencies.

- We accept each other irrespective of gender, ethnic background or church affiliation.
- We desire to work in multi-national teams and are committed to effective international cooperation.
- We recognise the importance of research and responding to God's directions for advance.
- We believe in full participation and oneness in decision making.
- We value servant leaders who wait on God for vision and direction.
- We promote local and innovative strategies through decentralised decision making.
- We make no appeals for funds.

If Jesus Christ be God and died for me,
no sacrifice can be too great for me
to make for Him.

C. T. Studd

www.wec-int.org

About the Author

Born in Brazil in 1966, Ronaldo Lidorio is an ordained pastor of the Presbyterian Church of Brazil. He has a BA in Theology and a PhD in Cultural Anthropology. He joined WEC International in 1992, and from 1993 to 2001 he was engaged in church planting and Bible translation among the Konkomba-Bimonkpeln people of north-eastern Ghana. Since 2002 he and his wife Rossana have been leading the WEC team in the Amazon, Brazil. Their focus is on evangelism, missionary training and church planting. They have two children, Vivian and Junior.